Unwritten Rules

Real Strategies to Parent Your Child into a Successful Adult

Adam Russo, LCSW

Unwritten Rules: Real Strategies to Parent Your Child into a Successful Adult
© 2017 by Adam Russo

ISBN: 978-0-9994403-0-8
Library of Congress Control Number: 2017916426

Printed in USA by Adam Russo

The publisher has strived to be as accurate and complete as possible in the creation of this book.

Disclaimer
Emotional and behavioral health is challenging to address and there certainly is no 'one size fits all' approach. In no way does the writer believe that what is written are the only intervention strategies to use when parenting children.

Any and all advice given throughout this book should be viewed through the lens of one's individual circumstances; some advice may not apply directly to your situation. The intent of the advice is for the reader to identify with parts that may be applicable to his or her life, and to use the advice offered in the ways that he or she best sees fit.

The intent of the stories contained herein is to create a situation with which many parents can identify in their own homes. This book is written with fictional stories portraying fictional characters. Any resemblance to actual persons or their lives is completely coincidental.

If there are situations occurring in your life or in the lives of your immediately family that are overwhelming you and feel impossible to manage, you are encouraged to consider seeking professional help. For more information, visit: https://www.adamrussobooks.com.

Dedication

This book is dedicated to my parents, who were wise to realize that results aren't everything.

And my family, for supporting me in this project.

Acknowledgements

I would like to thank Lisa Xagas and Abigaile VanHorn, PhD, for serving as my "beta readers". After giving much of their personal time and energy to reading the unedited draft, they provided invaluable and honest feedback which only enhanced the final product.

And thank you to my wife, Heather, for helping me generate ideas when I was out of them.

A Special Gift from Adam Russo

Now that you have your copy of *Unwritten Rules: Real Strategies to Parent Your Child to Success*, you can now feel secure that there is more than just test scores that determine the success of your child. It is a great benefit to be reinforced that *WHO* a child is, not what they accomplish, still matters.

You'll also receive a special bonus I created to add to your toolkit. It is a special bonus chapter that highlights the struggles that exist for kids who have a desire to focus on STEM (Science, Technology, Engineering, and Math), and how to combat them.

There's so much confusing information out there about parenting. When you finish this book you'll be armed with what you need to know to see through the "noise" and focus on the issues that really matter to you, as the parent.

You can claim your special bonus for free here:

https://www.adamrussobooks.com/hiddenchapter

The sooner you know what the most important issues are for you, as the parent, to focus on with your child, the better your chances to raise your child into a successful adult.

I'm in your corner. Let me know if I can help further.

Best,

Adam Russo

Preface

I've been a clinical therapist for almost 20 years, and a business owner for about 15 years. Over time, I've had the opportunity to clinically work with hundreds of parents and children. Through my experience in speaking with many families who clearly work so hard to improve their emotional and home lives, I've noticed common trends that they all tend to exhibit either in major or minor ways.

Most parents speak about their desire for their kids to be "successful." In the short term, this means something different to most parents. For example, it could mean successfully thriving in academic, social, athletic, or artistic arenas. For many, all of the above.

In the long term, parents focus on these things because they are all similar in what they want in the long term for their children: Material wealth and happiness. And parents believe that success in the academic and other areas noted above is an essential first step to achieving the goal of material wealth.

The problem is, the line of thinking isn't true. The most successful and happy adults are ultimately the ones who have developed the skills to be adaptive and independent. They are able to control and understand their emotions, align their behaviors with how they feel, and operate freely in many different environments without having to change the core of who they are.

In this book I tell fictional stories that are similar to those I've heard from many parents over the years. They are not shocking, but have potentially severe consequences. The attitude that parents have in how they are going to address these situations has a direct impact in how well they are preparing their children for an independent and adaptive adulthood.

There are no "right" or "wrong" answers to parenting. The goal of this book is to provide a philosophical base to parents as they think about addressing situations that arise with their children. Again, while there is no 100 percent correct way of handling a situation, the driving philosophy you have as a parent will impact your own choices, emotions, and actions.

Every chapter is unique. Feel free to skip around and read what you believe may be most pertinent to you. However, there is some overlap from chapter to chapter. So there can be value in chapters that may initially be perceived to not be of pertinence.

Contents

Introduction

"Only Losers Get Fired, Right?"

"We're going to have to let you go."

Not the phrase I wanted to hear. After being employed in the highest leadership role of my career, that was what I heard after just under a year with the organization. And I definitely didn't believe it was fair.

I was hired to be the Director of Youth Programs at a not-for-profit which provided residential services to adolescents who were wards of the state. The program was responsible for over forty children living in seven homes. These children had extreme emotional and behavioral difficulties. My professional background to that point had more than prepared me for the role, and I was excited to tackle it.

One of the homes was described to me as having historically major problems for the organization before I was hired. Many of those same issues existed when I started. I was aware of the problem, though not of the extent and severity of the issues.

I believed I did everything right. I didn't shy away from the difficult meetings with our organization's leadership, or the leadership at the state level who provided oversight of our agency. I ensured the action plans for improvement were followed. I advocated for more thorough reviews of all children who were recommended to be placed at that particular home if their needs were too extreme for our care. I even pushed our leadership to close down that particular home for 90 days so we could get our feet back under us and start over. All other aspects of the program were performing well, but this home still had major problems to resolve. It became apparent that, without a clean slate, they would never be fixed.

But then a funny thing happened. None of it mattered. It didn't matter that I was incredibly well respected in my previous positions, or that I had a number of successes in the short period of time I was in my role as Director, which included the successful expansion of many programs. No, what mattered was that the organization had to prove to the state they were doing something to fix the problem at this one particular home. They didn't want to lose the contract, so I was removed.

It was a position I never thought I'd be in. Only losers get fired, right? If someone gets laid off or fired, clearly they didn't bring the level of value the organization required. If they did, they'd still have a job...right? After success at every level of my career to that point, this was an outcome that I never thought would happen. This was a professional punch to the gut.

Personally, I was lucky, or smart, or both... I'm not completely sure. I received great advice from a physician with whom I worked some years earlier. He said, "Never put your eggs in one basket," with regards to income. What he meant was always have multiple areas where income can be generated because you never know what may happen to your primary source. I had taken his advice four years earlier and started a small, outpatient counseling agency. At the time, there were a few other therapists working there and we worked with a fair amount of people from the community. But it was nothing close to providing my family a living wage. I had dreamed of one day going to work for myself, but never did I think the choice would be made for me. Now, having an option to turn to was better than the alternative of having nothing.

My wife and I already spoke about the possibility of me losing my regular job because of the tone that had been developing in the workplace. She was more than supportive when it came to next steps, and I believed we had a good plan. What I wasn't prepared for was the feeling I would have when I came home after I was let go, having my kids run up to me and give a hug like they always did, oblivious (as they should be) to the realities that were now occurring. Don't losers get fired? I didn't want to be a loser dad.

That was an interesting weekend. We spoke about our financial status, and essentially crossed our fingers that working hard would solve all problems. As big *Seinfeld* fans, we recalled the episode where George wasn't sure if he was hired for a job, and couldn't reach the person who hired him. So he just showed up. He went to his office, ate crackers, sharpened pencils, and pretended to look busy. We joked that I would go into the office of my fledgling counseling agency and sharpen pencils all day.

Fast forward to now, nine years after this event, and it was the best thing that could have professionally happened to me. My fledgling counseling practice has turned into a large and well-respected agency with over 60 employees. Never in my wildest dreams did I think that would happen. And I don't believe it would have if I didn't have to experience hard, professional failure.

From the beginning, I did want to eventually work for myself... EVENTUALLY. No real plan, but I figured I'd know when it would be a good time. Things would *feel* right. So I waited. The agency was growing and looking good, but all I could see were the future costs and roadblocks. I played it safe and stayed employed with the larger, "safer" organizations. I tricked myself into thinking that a large system could provide assurances that I just couldn't provide myself on my own. The illusion of a consistent salary, benefits, vacation time, etc. were all things that existed. But what I wasn't thinking was that they could be taken away for no reason. I was operating under the rationale that I spoke about above, which was that "only losers get fired." Well, I wasn't a loser and performed my job responsibly and with integrity. Therefore, I saw security and predictability in my role.

When the choice was made for me to work for myself, I was scared. All of the things that I saw in the past as a barrier to success still existed, and no amount of reframing, encouragement, motivation, or drive could make those barriers go away. So I did the only thing I could. I worked (desperately) to remove the barriers. Looking back, I'm not sure how I did it. All I know is that I did the math and knew that for me to support my family, the agency had to bill a certain number of hours each week. We were about 60 percent short of that goal when I walked into the office on day one. I wanted to hit that goal in 30 days. If we could be at that level, I could see the barriers begin to shrink.

It was strange walking into that office the first day. The staff there knew I was coming since I had kept them up to speed on my situation. But we all spoke about how weird it was for them to see me there during the day as I always arrived in the evening. As supportive as they were for my situation, since "only losers get fired," I didn't know if they lost confidence in my ability to lead this small counseling practice. There were many other professional options for them, and I wasn't sure that any of them would stay. Having a leader who just lost a job doesn't exactly scream competency to a team of people. But we did hit the billed hours goal within the identified timeframe. And the rest is history.

I reflect on this because the purpose of this book to talk about the value of negative emotions and negative experiences. Too many times we dismiss the negative because it hurts too much or causes outcomes that are harmful. True, there are some experiences that are too painful to ever try to construe them as being positive or being a part of character development. But there are countless, difficult things that happen to us each and every day that we should be using to challenge our existing perspectives and using them as opportunities to learn.

But here's the thing: Our culture is changing our perspective for the worse. We are pressed, whether we realize it or not, to be happy and perfect. It's why countless studies conclude that the more active one is on social media, the higher the likelihood of that person to experience depression.

Our culture, attitudes, and perspectives are being shaped in a culture that values "instant happiness," "instant success." These things don't exist, yet our culture wants us (needs us?) to believe that it's true. As adults, we must wrap our minds around how we will process and understand this phenomenon. If we fall victim to it, not only will we suffer, but our children will as well.

Most of my story isn't uncommon: Adult has job, adult works hard, adult has success, adult loses job through no fault of their own, adult has to pick up the pieces. These things are getting harder for adults to manage. Through social media and societal pressures, the intensity of "keeping up with the Joneses" has created a far fall off the pedestal for those who have to go through this experience today. And people do fall… hard. The negative experiences in life don't stop. Losing a job is just an example. Whether it's a substantial medical issue, financial difficulties, marriage difficulties, substance use, gambling, or some other issue, there are hundreds of negative experiences and consequences that millions of people have to manage each and every day. Our culture makes it harder for us to fight the fight.

As adults keep these perspectives in their life, they believe the same should be true in the lives of their children. So they believe that preschool aged children should begin training for their life as a professional athlete. Or they push their children to overachieve academically with the belief that an Ivy League education will guarantee them success into adulthood. **Adults are pushing their kids down roads where they believe their kids will experience success the fastest with the least amount of hardship and to be "winners."**

Many adults do this, and it's a complete paradox with no good outcome for the children. Success is inherently slow and hard in achieving. We see the Mark Zuckerbergs of the world and say, "Why not my kid?" A billionaire at 26 (or whatever age he is), that would be a good life. Of course it would be. But if it was that easy, then everyone should be doing it. The reality is that most kids will grow up to be:

Average.

Yes, average. And our job as parents is to prepare them for their average life. I certainly believe kids should be pushed to achieve and learn all they can. But let's face it: In the end, they'll graduate high school or college (maybe graduate school), and be average. We spend more time preparing them for a life of greatness that they will most likely never, ever achieve, than preparing them for their average life full of problems and disappointments.

We, as parents, don't want them to have that average life. We know too well how hard that life is and we want something better for them. But we adults have to come to terms with the facts. We can't eliminate problems from our kids' lives and they'll do better by being better prepared to manage them, rather than us preparing them to have no problems at all.

Parents try to prepare their children for this 'better life' by following any advice they can obtain through schools, coaches, tutors, parenting books, or family members. Parents are looking for the roadmap to follow in order to guarantee that their kids will be 'successful' in adulthood. But there is no map. There are no rules.

As parents, we intrinsically know that our children will inevitably face hardships, challenges, and struggles. The real question is "How equipped will they be to handle them"?

It is the unwritten rules, ones that are not often spoken about, that cultivate the perseverance, empathy, and grit, that can turn children into successful adults. And embracing this truth will help parents best prepare their kids for their futures.

But average isn't bad. It's just hard. And because it's hard, there are character traits that are essential to have in order to thrive in an "average" life. Throughout this book, I'll talk about how to best prepare your kids for their real adult lives that will be challenging, exciting, nerve-wracking, disappointing, and tragic... all emotions that the average human, all humans, will experience. As adults, we all know these things will be true, so let's open our minds to teaching our kids the skills they need and create an adaptive and independent future generation.

Chapter 1

The Rat Race

The Story

"Put the damn phone away!" Bonnie was really frustrated at her 13-year old son, Mike.

She and her husband, Tony, gave Mike the phone two years ago. There were no issues at the beginning. But over the last few months, Mike seemed completely consumed by whatever was occurring on the screen. Tony and Bonnie had tried to mitigate the effects on Mike. But currently they feel like they are losing the battle.

"Just one more second, mom. I don't know why you're getting all worked up. Geez," Mike said, never looking up.

"I've asked you a thousand times already. I am not waiting another second," Bonnie was going to lose her mind.

"Fine!" Mike yelled and slammed the phone down on the kitchen table. "Are you happy now?" He retorted sarcastically and stormed off to his room.

Bonnie and Tony hated these confrontations that they had with their son, but saw them as necessary evils if they wanted to set limits with his time on screens.

They talked with each other about how times have changed. Technology is now a large part of an adolescent's life. The change in times is very different than how Bonnie and Tony grew up, and they knew they weren't the only parents struggling to manage their teenagers with this issue.

As much as they knew that technology had its benefits (they could communicate with Mike when they were both at work, for example), they were concerned about what they didn't know. They didn't know how much time Mike was spending on his phone after school and while they were still at work. They certainly didn't know what was so important that he had to engage with his phone all the time. Tony would speak about articles he read about communication apps where the messages or videos would disappear from a phone after they were read, and how kids were invested in getting 'likes' on the things that they would post on different social media sites.

Tony and Bonnie felt like the technology (beyond Facebook) was over their heads and couldn't understand how all of this worked, or how it affected their son. What they did know was that Mike was spending too much time on his phone, and they assumed that all of the potential problems that they had read about were becoming a problem for him.

But overall it hadn't become too large of a problem. Mike seemed to have a decent group of friends, good grades, and was a great athlete. Bonnie and Tony wanted to encourage Mike to be as engaged in school, friends, and sports as they could, and did push him to excel. Unspoken, Bonnie and Tony agreed some time ago that because Mike was able to maintain a high level of success in multiple areas of his life, they were going to not be too hard on him. After all, they did want to push him academically and athletically, and thought that he should have time to himself.

Bonnie figured that she would let Mike be for now. She was working from home today and thought she should get something productive done, but felt like she needed to decompress first. There were many items that they needed at home: Mike needed some shirts, Tony wanted some new "toys" for his grill, and she needed some new shoes. Bonnie went online and found the best prices for all of the items. Of course, Mike's and Tony's things would be able to arrive the next day, but she would have to wait five days for her shoes. That was frustrating for her. Bonnie had ordered many things online in the past and had grown accustomed to her items arriving the next day.

She decided to check her own Facebook page and see what information she could glean from the neighborhood. Bonnie was surprised to find a new football camp was starting in the next few weeks, and it was being led by the head coach at the local high school. This was a huge opportunity for Mike, and she was surprised that he didn't say anything about it. There was time to register. So she decided that given the events of the day, she would wait to address this with him until the time was right.

As she continued to scroll down her page, she was saddened to see that women in her neighborhood appeared to get together a couple of nights ago for dinner. In looking at the pictures, she was surprised she wasn't invited, as she was friends with many of them. While Bonnie didn't consider herself insecure, seeing this picture did elicit feelings of anxiety as she was suddenly worried that maybe she wasn't as good of friends with many of these people as she thought. Bonnie dismissed this thought and told herself to remember about the football camp for Mike.

Later that night, she spoke with Tony about what happened with Mike earlier in the day. Mike had since grabbed his phone and was using it again.

"I just don't know what to do," Tony was exasperated. "No matter how many times we tell him to put it down and do something productive, he doesn't. And we can't take it away from him because we need to contact him during the day."

"You always say that. But we have a house phone. There are phones at school. We grew up without cell phones and we figured it out. I don't think we should be so quick to decide that we can't take his phone," Bonnie pushed back.

"But at least he tells us when he's home and doesn't leave us wondering where he is. Plus, his grades are good, so I don't want to be too hard on him," Tony was trying to figure out what the best, next step would be.

"He does do most of the things he should be doing, except for containing himself with that phone," Bonnie agreed. "Then what's our problem?"

Tony thought about it for a minute, but he didn't like the conclusion.

"Well, maybe it's that we know how dependent he is on using his phone. And we don't want to deal with what tantrum Mike will have when we do actually take it from him," Tony winced at his statement.

"I hate to say it, but I can't disagree with you," Bonnie was cringing at the thought.

"Maybe before we do something, we should try to understand what the value of the phone is to Mike rather than just judging his use," Tony shifted into his role at work as a Human Resource professional.

"Not a bad idea," Bonnie agreed.

"Maybe we should also look at how we use our phones, too, at least to try to understand what the problem really is," Tony added.

"All right, let's do it."

As the next few weeks went by, Bonnie and Tony began to notice that Mike's grades started dropping. Not enough to be a problem, but enough to notice. Further, they realized that he was spending less time with friends and more time alone in his room. When he did come out and join them, Mike was irritable and frustrated. One day around dinner time, Mike came downstairs and he was not in a good mood.

"Where's dinner. I'm hungry," Mike demanded.

Bonnie and Tony looked at each other, then back at Mike. He was a mess. Hair not combed, some food stains on his clothes, and they caught a whiff of BO from across the kitchen.

"It'll be ready in about 15 minutes," said his dad. "What have you been up to?"

"None of your business. I don't understand why you always want to know all about me," Mike already was reacting to his dad.

"Look, I don't know what the problem is, but your attitude has been nothing but poor over the past few weeks. Not to mention, we see your grades slipping, and you've just been holed up in your room. So don't give me this," Tony was getting angry.

"So now what I'm doing isn't good enough? I don't know what you want from me!" Mike was losing it.

"Just go to your room for a while. We'll talk about this later," Tony was trying to avoid a fight.

Mike again stormed upstairs. This time Tony and Bonnie jumped as they heard the loud slam of Mike's bedroom door.

"I think we need to take his phone," Bonnie was becoming more firm in this position.

"I'm still not sure. While I don't disagree with you, we haven't really spoken with Mike about what is going on. We're just dancing around the issue," Tony said in partial agreement.

"Well, we can't continue like this. What will it take for you to agree with me?"

"I don't know. Have you paid much attention to the value you get from your phone? I know I haven't," Tony replied.

"No, not really," said Bonnie.

"OK, let's commit, one week. Let's be conscious for one week about what we're doing with our phones. After that, we talk about it and make a decision about the best ways to move forward. Sound like a plan?" Tony found himself getting motivated by his idea.

"Done."

Tony didn't know what to expect from his week of self-examination. It took work to let some of his concern for Mike's behaviors go so he could really focus on what his own relationship was with technology. But he knew it was necessary in order to better understand what his son was going through, and why it was creating such struggles for him. Tony checked his emails and texts from friends and family, checked some sports scores and news, nothing all that interesting.

On Day Two of the week challenge, he visited his Facebook page. He scrolled through the page glancing at the many pictures and inspirational quotes that were posted. Then he came across an image that felt like he was punched in the gut. His brother was taking his family on another trip to Caribbean. This was the second time they had been there this year, on top of two other vacations they splurged on. Tony hated the emotions that this generated in him. He was jealous, felt inferior to his brother, and was ashamed at having both feelings. Yes, his brother should be able to do what he wanted since he was a successful corporate executive. Just because Tony chose a different path and didn't have the means of his brother, it didn't mean that his life was less successful. It only appeared to be. The last vacation post that Tony had was when they drove five hours to the nearest beach for a long weekend. Not the Caribbean, but it was as close as his family could get.

Day Three went mostly the same as Day Two. More emails, sports, news. More pictures from his brothers' vacation. Barf! The new post that he saw was about a football camp that was going to be starting in the next few months. He thought Mike would be interested in this. He thought it would also help Mike get out of his current funk.

Tony was scrolling through the comments on the football camp post and saw that many parents were taking this camp very seriously, as it was being led by the head coach at the local high school. Parents wrote that they had heard rumors that this camp was the "inside track" for eighth graders going into high school. If your kid wanted to play, they needed to register. Tony then read that a group of parents were going to register their sons for a "group training" session in the two weeks before the camp started. The parents' comments noted that they wanted to be sure that their sons were in the best shape possible for the camp, as it was the only opportunity they would have to showcase their talents for the coach, and they wanted to be sure that they took complete advantage of it.

Tony couldn't believe that parents were going to register their kids, essentially, to go to a camp to prepare for the actual camp. While he told himself that this ranked up there as one of the dumbest ideas he had ever heard, he couldn't help but wonder if he should be registering Mike for the camp as well. After all, Mike had been playing football for the past six years. How fair would it be to Mike if he didn't make the team in high school because his dad didn't want to spend the extra money and time to register him for the classes that would've prepared him for success? Tony didn't like this, but was beginning to feel like he had no other choice. He resolved to speak with Bonnie about it over the next week as there was plenty of time to decide next steps.

Days Four and Five were similar to previous days. More pictures of his brother's vacation (vomit), news, etc. Tony found himself frustrated that emails and texts he had sent both for personal and professional reasons had gone unanswered. He did need responses to these messages, and the frustration that people were not responding quickly was building. He was able to keep himself in check and decided to wait an extra couple of days before he reached out again.

He revisited his Facebook page and there continued to be more comments and thoughts about the upcoming football camp and the "pre-camp" that the parents had been speaking about. There seemed to me more parents on board with sending their kids to the pre-camp to prepare. Tony started to type a comment and share his conflicting thoughts about what parents were speaking about, but quickly decided against it. He knew that he would most likely be skewered for his perspective. The fight wasn't worth it.

As the week closed, it was more of the same for him. Tony was finally getting responses to the pressing questions he had asked of colleagues and friends, and it looked like his brother returned home from their trip (which made him feel better). He couldn't believe that parents were still posting thoughts about the upcoming football camp and the preparations that they were going to have their sons take in order to optimally perform. Now they were talking about protein shakes and other natural things to help their kids build strength and resist injury. The concern now was that if the kids went to the pre-camp, would they be at a greater risk of getting hurt during the actual camp, and how that would be devastating as the kids would lose their only opportunity.

Bonnie was curious about their experiment. She hated that they had seen the issues with Mike fester for as long as they had without action on their part as parents. But she did agree with Tony that gaining some insight into Mike's experience would be helpful. For as long as they had waited to strongly intervene, another week wasn't going to change anything.

Over the first couple of days, Bonnie spent time ordering things from various websites that they needed for their home. Bonnie wasn't as concerned with the price of the items, as much as she was trying to find who could get the item into her hands the fastest without spending extra shipping costs. She would also send some notes to friends, and try to do some research for a project for work. The research for work ate up much of the time she was spending online, and Bonnie began to question how valuable this experiment was going to be.

On Day Five, she visited her Facebook page, and immediately she wished she hadn't. As she scrolled through her posts, she recognized that there were a couple of other "girls nights" that had happened without her being invited. Bonnie again looked at the people who attended and couldn't believe that she wasn't asked. She started to feel sad and worried that maybe the friends she had weren't as friendly as she thought.

Those thoughts were put on pause as she moved onto a post just past the previous one. This post was referencing the football camp that she saw a week or so earlier. But this post had many comments from parents speaking about many topics from the camp, including getting the kids involved in a pre-camp training, protein shakes and nutritional supplements, and how to best get the coach's attention while at camp. Bonnie was overwhelmed by the post. She recognized many parents were using this camp as an opportunity for their kids to compete for a spot on the team prior to high school beginning, but had many mixed feelings about it. On the one hand she wanted to engage in the discussion. Bonnie didn't want Mike to be left out or not as good at something just because she couldn't handle the competitiveness of the discussion. And yet she was also frustrated because she thought sports should be fun and this level of intensity over eighth grade sports seemed like it was going too far.

Bonnie's work project consumed the remainder of her week and she never did revisit Facebook. She was happy that her items were delivered timely, as she hated when they came later than initially stated.

Mike continued to maintain his status quo over the course of the week. His grades stabilized, but never did improve, and he continued to spend a lot of time in his room. His attitude when conversing with his parents seemed to improve, but Bonnie and Tony surmised that this was because they weren't challenging him nearly has much as they had been over the previous week.

After the experiment was complete, Bonnie and Tony finally sat down to talk about their experience and to figure out what to do with Mike.

"OK, so, how was it?" Bonnie went first.

"A little surprising," said Tony. "I found that as helpful as being able to communicate electronically is for some things, it isn't really helpful for others. I liked being able to quickly ask people the questions that were essential for me, but hated having to wait for a response from them. And I don't know if you saw it, but there was this whole thing about an upcoming football camp that parents were getting all riled up about on Facebook. Reading those comment chains was really bothering me".

"I did see that!" Bonnie exclaimed. "Those parents were going nuts about the whole thing! Pre-camps and protein shakes, and how to best position their kids to get on the team. It was pretty sad reading all that. And I also realized that I wanted things to happen quickly and easily also, like when I order stuff for the house. If it can't be here in two days, I'll move on to another site that can be faster."

"I know, I thought the same thing. But to be honest, I couldn't help but wonder if we were missing out on the things we should be doing for Mike. I mean, I know it's crazy, but what if all these parents really follow through on what they're saying? What chance will Mike have?" Mike wondered.

"Reading what all these people post is hard. Like I saw that many of the women in the neighborhood went out together a few times over the past couple of weeks and I wasn't invited. I can't help but wonder if I was more active on Facebook, would they have remembered to ask me? And I'm frustrated that I even have to think that way. Do I need to be active on Facebook to maintain friendships?" Bonnie was at a loss.

"I'm sorry; I know you enjoy doing things with them. I had a similar experience. My brother took his family on another expensive vacation, and I hated seeing it," Tony admitted.

"Maybe what we need to acknowledge is that we get caught up on what we see online, especially in social media. Do you think it's possible that Mike is getting swallowed up in the same things?" asked Bonnie.

"Let's ask him," said Tony.

When Mike came down, he looked like he was prepared for an argument. He was surprised when his parents opened with a question rather than a declaration.

"We know we get on your case for spending so much time on your phone. But we'd like to know what you're spending your time doing, and why that is so important to you?" his mom gently asked.

"Well, I just talk to my friends, I guess. I mean, there's not much else going on."

"Just talk? Let's be honest, you tend to be really quiet up there. What are you really doing? There isn't a lot of talking," his dad pressed.

"Well, it's mostly chatting through messaging apps and other things. While I'm messaging people I'm also scrolling through different posts on Facebook, Instagram, and other things to 'like' and comment on what my friends post."

"I get the messaging, but why the scrolling of posts in those other apps?" asked his mom.

"If I don't 'like' things and stay active, people may leave me out of a conversation that I want to be involved in. And if someone is really proud of something that they do, or posts something really cool, they get angry if people don't 'like' it right away."

"I'm a little confused. Do you stay on your phone because you like to or because you feel like you have to?" This question from Tony was directed towards Mike, but it strongly resonated with all three of them.

"A little of both, but more because I have to, I guess. When I'm online I can see the pictures of parties and things I'm missing out on, and I'm trying to stay involved so I can maybe get invited to other things."

Bonnie and Tony couldn't argue with Mike. He was making sense. And the good news was they were all staying calm and listening to each other.

"But you see that your grades are slipping right? And your attitude around here hasn't been the greatest," said Bonnie.

"I do. I've told myself I have to put my phone down more often, but I can't seem to be able to. I get angry when you tell me to because I'd like to be able to do it myself."

"Are you worried that you'll miss out on what other people are doing if you don't engage with them?" asked Tony.

"Yeah."

"Well, would it make you feel any better if you knew that your mom and I have a hard time with the same things?"

"What do you mean?"

"Do you know about that football camp that's coming up?" Mike nodded. "Your mom and I have been reading tons of posts from parents about all the things that they are going to do to best prepare their kids for this camp. They're putting a lot of weight on this camp and believe it's like a 'make-or-break' for playing in high school. Your mom and I have been unsure about what to do next. We don't want you to miss out on this opportunity."

"You could have just asked me. I know all these kids are doing a class beforehand, or whatever. I don't want to do that. I just want to go to the camp and have fun."

They spoke much more that evening, and agreed that the extent they were spending time in social media was making things worse for all of them. Mike especially was able to state that the more he worried about things socially, the harder it was to focus on schoolwork, and his grades suffered for it. As a family, they agreed to take a two-week break from social media, decompress, and then see what would be best for them individually after the two weeks were over.

The Lesson

While the technological advancements in our culture have been great, they are eating up many families. The ease with which we can engage in commerce, obtain information, or learn about virtually any topic is unprecedented and extremely convenient. We are able to do things that the generations before us never would have thought possible. You may remember that 10 to 15 years ago, if you had to place an order to have an item shipped to your home, you would be told that it would take four to six weeks. If it arrived in three weeks, you would be thrilled. Today, we like it when things arrive the next day. Maybe we can handle within seven days (depending on the item), but anything longer than a week is frustrating.

I remember that in high school, it was hard to make plans with friends. For example, if it was a Saturday and I wanted to hang out with friends that night, but my parents wanted me to go somewhere with them during the day, I had to wait to reach my friends until I returned home. And then I had to call them from my home phone and hope that they were home so they could answer the phone. Eventually we would all connect, but at times it was a one- to two-hour process just to make contact.

Fast forward to now and virtually every high school student has a cell phone. There is no waiting for contact with the person they want to reach. Students are able to connect instantaneously with whomever they would like through all types of messaging apps and social media platforms.

The same thing is occurring with parents. Adults are getting involved in social media platforms as way to stay in touch with family and friends who live far away, or to get engaged and involved with local friends or organizations. What occurs very often is that many adults and kids are not prepared for how to manage the downside of these technological advancements, and that's what happened in the story.

In the story, we had two parents and a teenager struggling to manage the effects of social media and the instantaneous nature of communication and technology. Being unable to manage these things created a chain reaction of issues that occurred for the family at home. In the story, the family was able to regain its footing by slowing down and examining why these issues were occurring. Sadly, many families are not able to do this, and instead continue to double down on the actions that were creating negative consequences. They believe that there really is a way to "win" the social media and communication game. Sadly, there is not.

Many studies have come to the conclusion that heavy social media use has an adverse effect on the individuals, especially young people, who engage in it. A University of Pittsburgh School of Medicine Study (2016) summarized its findings well: Those who engage heavily in Facebook have "highly idealized representations of peers on social media which elicits feelings of envy and the distorted belief that others lead happier, more successful lives." Similar findings have been replicated across many studies, and yet parents continue to allow their children free rein with regards to their social media use.

This seems to be due to parents not wanting their children to miss out on what may be occurring with their friends. Parents are extremely concerned with the social consequences that their children may experience because they are also conscious of this experience in their own lives. When parents feel the anxiety as it relates to social media, they will also be acutely aware of the social pressures that their kids face, and are reluctant to set limits because of the "panic" that may be created in the child. Parents hate feeling like they are the cause of their children's anxiety. They are therefore reluctant to set limits with social media because they believe the adverse effects are disproportionate to the behavior. Parents just want their kids to lay off the phone for a while, not destroy their social lives. The problem is that kids feel that it will destroy their social lives, and parents typically acquiesce to the child because they don't want to cause more problems.

Just like everything else, social media can be a good thing, but only if used in moderation. It becomes a problem when people feel like their lives are horrible because they really do believe the "idealized representations" that they see posted. Further, they then believe everyone else (whoever that is) is doing "better" things than they are, and are "exceptional." The cognitive distortions snowball to a point to where an individual now has created a reality based on images that they see and posts they read. Somehow they compare their own reality to these images and it's always worse than what they see. Young people are especially susceptible to this, which is why panic sets in when they can't engage with social media. They do not see the average lives that their friends lead, yet "average" is what we all are.

The Instant Culture

This situation highlights the negative factors of the "instant" culture that we live in now. With instant communication, instant news, and instant images, young people are being programmed to expect good things to happen instantly. While that's not a problem if they want to download music right away or order an item to arrive the next day, it is a problem when it comes to forming relationships or working towards a goal. Delayed gratification is essential to success, and culturally we are not embedding this trait in our young people as much as we should be.

A landmark study performed at Stanford University by Walter Mischel in the late 1960s to early 70s (known as the "marshmallow experiment") highlighted the correlation to delayed gratification and success. In short, the researchers had young children (kindergarten age) sit at a table with a marshmallow in front of them. The children were told that the researcher would leave the room, and while they were gone, they could eat the marshmallow. But, if they didn't eat the marshmallow and were able to wait until the researcher returned, they would receive more marshmallows to eat. Some kids were successful, others were not. The researchers then followed the kids' success for four to five decades afterward. They found that the children who were able to wait to eat the marshmallow had higher standardized test scores, lower rates of substance use, lower rates of obesity, and less reported emotional and medical issues.

Why does this matter? While our culture becomes more "instant," the things that lead to success haven't changed. It still takes hard work, determination, motivation, failure, and perseverance to be successful. No matter how convenient our culture becomes, or how many barriers get removed in order to streamline processes to make our lives easier, or how many devices are created to help us be productive, being able to delay gratification will be essential to success in any field. Can you imagine what would've happened if Thomas Edison quit trying to invent a light bulb? It was reported he had about 1000 failed experiments before he was successful. When asked how it felt to fail 1,000 times, he replied, "I didn't fail 1000 times. The light bulb was an invention with 1000 steps." Delayed gratification indeed.

As parents we continue to expect things should be easy for our kids because the changes that have occurred during this technological revolution dictate that everything should be easier. We've come upon an era of convenience so speak. Parents believe that their children shouldn't have to struggle academically, socially, athletically, artistically, or otherwise. If they just took a class or obtained a tutor, the problem should be solved. But parents are incredulous if their child attends a sports camp and still doesn't make their team of choice. Or maybe they enrolled their child in the best SAT prep course around, only to see an insignificant improvement in their scores.

Parents now expect the best should happen quickly and easily for their kids. This is the biggest hoax that parents project onto kids today. Life does not happen easily. Or successfully. I would guarantee that every single person you know has, had, or will have a significant hardship in their lives. They are impossible to avoid, yet we raise our kids with the "instant" culture belief system that they will be able to avoid it. As long as they say, do, and act the right way, there will be no issues. Parents sell the idea that there is a formula to completely avoid adversity even when no such formula exists. And this is how our culture perpetrates this greatest travesty on our kids. Rather than teaching that life is hard and challenging, we're teaching not only that it shouldn't be, but that there's a way to beat it.

Too Much Focus on the Outcome

School systems, athletic departments, and other institutions have colluded in this belief as well. What's being sold to kids is that as long as they are "the best," then they can beat adversity. "The best" don't have struggles. Their lives are full of bliss and fun. It's why we see parents entering preschool age kids into extremely competitive soccer leagues, why high school students overload themselves with AP classes, why people believe where they attend college actually matters (we'll speak about this in a later chapter), and why many parents cannot accept a less than optimal outcome that their child has on a given endeavor, even though they worked incredibly hard. In all of these examples, the children, parents, teachers, and coaches are focused on the outcome. Did you win? What was your grade? When focused solely on outcomes, kids miss the point of everything.

If a child really wants to get an A in a class, the value isn't in whether he actually gets the A. That's a result. The value is in the process of obtaining the A, how committed were they, how hard did they work. It's why I believe that kids who get straight As without having to study are at a disadvantage compared to the kids who have to work hard to earn Bs. The hard-working B students are practicing how to deal with and manage adversity without a perfect outcome at the end. This process mirrors life. It's great that the other students can get the As, but they need to practice managing adversity in their lives otherwise they will be ill-prepared for the future.

And what about those students who work incredibly hard to earn their As? I would want them to be able to handle a B. I have worked with too many high school students over the years who study incredibly hard to do the best they are able to in school, yet have been unable to emotionally manage anything less than an A in their classes. They believe they have fallen short, are scared of the future academic consequences, and struggle to allow themselves to appreciate their hard work and diligence even though the outcome wasn't what they wanted. And many of these kids struggle to manage anxiety. They get preoccupied with many things. They believe they really can control outcomes of situations by their hard work. While this is somewhat true as it relates to school, it's not true in life. Hard work doesn't solve all issues, and there must be an acceptance that no matter how hard one may work at accomplishing the right things, the wrong things can and will happen eventually.

Because of all of these factors, it is imperative for parents to take an active role in managing the culture for their kids. Before the turn of the century, practicing delayed gratification was simply embedded in our culture. Communication, information gathering, commerce, etc. all took forever. Now that many functions of our day-to-day lives can happen quickly, it's incumbent on parents to teach kids to… wait. If your child wants a new video game, do you buy it for them? Or, do you make them earn it through chores? If your child wants more than anything to be a good basketball player, but after practicing for three minutes in the driveway, returns inside sulking because they haven't yet made a basket, do you only console them? Or do you empathize with the struggle and make sure they go out and keep trying? If your 10-year old is watching TV and asks if you can get him or her a drink, what do you do? While it may be not be a big deal for you to get it, you should encourage kids to get it on their own.

It's hard to be a parent. With the push to always positively reinforce kids, teaching them delayed gratification is doubly challenging. As parents, we must tune out the "noise" (as I like to call it), and simply focus on teaching our kids the principles and values that are important to our respective families, rather than worrying about what everyone else will think about us. Engaging in this style of parenting will best set our children up to be adaptive and independent into the future.

Chapter 2

Humble Pie

The Story

"I can't believe he did it again!"

Helen was completely bewildered. The school year was more than halfway complete and her nine-year old son, Scott, had again left his completed homework assignment square in the middle of the their kitchen table. Helen and her husband, John, had spent more than enough nights coaching, coaxing, and cajoling their son into forming a routine so he could always have the things he needed for school the next day, including homework.

It all started innocently enough. The second week of school, Helen realized that Scott had forgotten his homework at home. So she did what "good" parents are supposed to do: She grabbed a pair of flip-flops and her car keys, and drove to his school as quickly as she could. Helen knew that Scott had worked very hard on this assignment. And with it being the second week of school, she didn't want him to lose points for not turning it in on time.

Further, she knew Scott would be very worried about not having it to turn in. How well could he focus if he didn't have it? Bringing the assignment to school fixed many problems. Scott could both get well-deserved full credit on his assignment, and it would also put his mind at ease. And Helen also felt great about herself as a parent for taking such good care of her child.

As the school year progressed, these incidents continued. The first few times, Helen didn't flinch. If she saw forgotten homework or an occasional lunch, she'd zip down to the school to drop it off (after all, it was right down the street). After the fourth time, Helen and John began to more actively work with Scott to stay organized. Scott was a typical nine-year old boy, losing attention in boring topics after about seventeen seconds of discussion. Instead, he would begin thinking about how the Jedi-led Rebels could overthrow the Empire in an even more interesting way than the last time (which once included flushing Darth Vader down the toilet).

Helen and John saw some progress, but not a lot. The progress would occur in the short time after a "talk." But after a week or two, Scott would revert to his past behaviors. They then tried to reward him when he remembered to bring everything to school, and take something away from him if he forgot something at home. But they just couldn't always remember to follow through. This resulted in frustration between the parents for not being able to put together a plan that worked. As well, the inconsistency of the rewards and consequences were not influencing Scott's behaviors at all.

Because of the inconsistency and frustration, Helen and John had told Scott in a vague way that if he couldn't remember to pack his things for school, neither of his parents would bring them to school for him anymore. They kept this threat vague because neither of them could (wanted to?) commit to follow through with it. They hoped the lingering fear that it was something that could happen would be enough of a deterrent to scare Scott into compliance.

Helen and John thought about Scott in similar ways. He was their only child and they loved him very much. They viewed parenting as a great responsibility and wanted nothing but the best for him. They didn't want him to feel bad things. They thought that the more things in his life that could go in a positive direction, the better he would be.

Scott followed the rules most of the time, he didn't misbehave at school, was always great at friends' homes, and adults always had nice things to say about him. Teachers would describe him as being "mature" for his age and other parents praised his social skills. While Helen and John were very proud of Scott, they couldn't understand why organizing himself was so difficult.

About a week later, Scott forgot three things at home: Homework, music instrument, and more homework. It was the last forgotten homework assignment that made Helen snap. Later that night, the three of them discussed the issue.

"Seriously Scott! How in the world does this continue to happen? What is the problem? Tell me. What is the problem?!" Helen was furious

"I just forgot, mom. It's not a big deal."

"Not a big deal?! It happens time and time and time again. Every day, I have to go to the school to drop off whatever you forgot to bring! It's tiring. And what makes me so angry is that you don't seem to appreciate it!" Helen was on a roll.

"Mom, everyone's parents bring stuff in if they forget it. I don't think everyone else's parents are getting as worked up as you are."

"Scott, I don't care what everyone else is doing. I care about what you're doing. And what you're doing is completely irresponsible!"

"I agree with your mom. She is trying to work with you and help you, but you're not making it any easier," John interjected.

"Dad, you don't get it. I do try but it's just not that big of a deal."

"Scott, you're leaving us no choice," said his mom. "If you don't think it's that big of a deal, and you're not going to take it seriously, then maybe next time I won't bring to school what you left at home. We're four months into the school year and you should be on track with getting your stuff together for school. I shouldn't have to look over your shoulder at every step."

"And Scott, you're not asking for help with organizing your things," said his dad. "If you were, it would be easier to work with you as you figured it out. But your inability to take this seriously is really infuriating."

Scott looked blankly past his mom and dad. His parents hoped that he heard some of this, but they still weren't convinced that he did.

"Scott," his mom put her arms around his shoulders and he looked at her. "We just can't keep doing the same thing over and over and expect something different to happen. The next time you leave something home, you're on your own. I can't save you."

"This is so unfair!" Scott shouted. "Other kids' parents want to help them. All you want to do is make my life miserable!"

"Scott, we know you're upset," said his dad, "but you'll never learn how to be responsible if we keep doing things in the same ways. You're mom's right."

Helen and John consoled him, reminded him that they loved him, but stood by their commitment to eliminate the extra trip to school no matter how important the item at home was to Scott.

But he did it again.

And this was the most important assignment Scott has had to complete so far: A large packet of math problems that Scott had spent hours on, meticulously working to ensure that he knew the answers to all of them. Scott wasn't a perfectionist by any stretch, but he took a particular ownership on this assignment and was proud of the work he had done once completed.

Scott left it on the kitchen table as he grabbed his bag like he always did. Even though Helen asked him if he had everything (she really wanted him to) and he obliged with a "Yes, mom!", somehow she was left looking at three perfectly stapled pages of math problems on her kitchen table.

Helen was beside herself. She called John, hoping that he would be able to rationalize her into going to the school to support Scott, and then they could both justify their rationale later that night. But John wasn't picking up his phone. Helen knew the importance of a parent being consistent and following through on what they say to their kids. Scott forgetting necessary items at home had become such a prevalent issue, she couldn't pretend the threat wasn't made. She tried to though. Helen thought about any way to not follow through on what she said.

The more Helen thought about it, she realized that she didn't care about Scott's grade if he didn't have his assignment, or if the teacher would be frustrated. She was incredibly worried about how Scott would feel if he didn't have it. Would he be the only one? Would he cry? Would he be so anxious that he would vomit? And after school, would he talk to her? Would he be so mad that he couldn't trust her? Helen wanted her son to trust her.

But what was trust? If she didn't follow through on the ultimatum, she knew that Scott wouldn't trust her when she made other ones in the future. If she did, Scott may be upset, but he could trust that she would follow through. Helen wasn't totally sure why this mattered.

It was 9:15 a.m. The packet of math problems didn't move. Helen started doing things around the house to distract herself. She was fearful that if she got in the car, somehow the math problems would, too, and then she would end up at the school.

11:30 a.m. Helen wasn't sure about her decision. There was still time to drop it off. She was scared that Scott wouldn't be able to manage this level of stress. After all, he was only nine. Maybe they were being too hard on him.

1:00 p.m. The school day was almost over. Helen had come to terms with her decision. She believed that if developing trust was important, then Scott needed to know that she would follow through with whatever the plan was.

At 2:30 p.m., Helen drove to the school to pick Scott up at the end of the day. She was nervous about how Scott would act, but still confident in her decision. Scott opened the door, threw his bag down on the back seat and slammed the car door. He was visibly upset and clearly had cried at some (multiple?) point that day. Helen asked how he was. Scott remained silent. They remained silent during the three-minute ride back home.

When they walked in, Helen held up the assignment that Scott had forgotten and asked, "How was your day?"

Scott was mad.

"IT'S ALL YOUR FAULT! THE OTHER KIDS MADE FUN OF ME BECAUSE I COULDN'T STOP CRYING! IF YOU HAD ONLY BROUGHT MY HOMEWORK TO SCHOOL NONE OF THIS WOULD HAVE HAPPENED!"

Helen tried to console him, but it wasn't working. He was angry and sobbing at the same time. Helen didn't know what to do. Eventually Scott stomped upstairs and slammed the door to his room. Helen was upset. She had never seen Scott like that before. She felt as though she let him down. As much as she told herself that wasn't true, she couldn't help thinking that she was wrong. Helen did remind herself that this shouldn't have been a surprise to Scott. She and John told him this is exactly what would happen should he forget something again, as they were tired of bailing him out. If Scott didn't like the consequences, he should have remembered his homework. That was her rationale.

Later that night, Helen and John went to talk to Scott about the events of the day. Scott calmed down, though he was still angry. Helen and John spoke to him about the importance of accountability and the fact that even if he didn't like how he felt now, someday he would understand why it was important.

They also talked about how the purpose wasn't to embarrass him in front of his friends, or get him in trouble with his teacher. They talked about how in life there are always consequences to actions, and he has to be prepared to deal with the consequences of his actions, regardless of whether the outcome is positive or negative. Scott didn't appear as though he heard this or could appreciate it, but at least wasn't arguing.

The next day Scott woke up in a much better mood, but still not back to what his mom would call "normal." He ate breakfast, went to school, and the days went on like they always did. It wasn't until about five weeks later that Helen realized Scott hadn't forgotten a homework assignment since the blowup occurred.

The Lesson

As parents, we think we get the point, but we don't. We think the point is about the short term. But the reality is that the goal of any intervention is always a long term focus.

In the story, Helen and John were focused strictly on the short-term behavior: Scott remembering to bring all necessary items to school each day. While this is a worthy focus, the interventions that Helen and John used were not working. All they wanted as parents was compliance. If Scott would only comply with what was expected of him, Helen and John could relax. But when Scott didn't comply, when things did get difficult, Helen and John ran out of options. Rather, they ran out of options that they were *comfortable* implementing and had to do something that made them feel uncomfortable.

Let's examine this intervention a little more closely so we can understand the real ramifications of their choice.

Intervention: Not saving Scott. Helen didn't bring work to school and allowed Scott to accept natural consequences of his actions.

First Outcome: Scott had to deal with the natural consequences of his choices. In all the times Scott had forgotten assignments, instruments, etc., he had not yet been forced to accept the consequences of his actions and be held to account. Simply put, no matter what his parents did, he didn't become any more motivated to comply with their requests to be better prepared for school. When Helen decided not to save him, it was the first time he had to experience consequences from another source: His teacher and classmates. This was a different experience for him and created a strong emotional reaction from Scott.

Second Outcome: This emotional reaction was different than the ones he would experience with his parents. Scott most likely would feel a little bit of guilt for forgetting his work, a little anxious because he didn't know how his teacher would react, a little shame because he had spoken with his parents about it so much, and he probably knew he should have remembered.

Today, parents work tremendously hard to have their kids not feel feelings like shame, guilt, embarrassment, fear, and anxiety. But there is great value to kids learning these emotions. Because Scott didn't yet have the experience of feeling these things, it was overwhelming to him. He was mad that his mom "put him in that position" and felt as though she should have "saved" him. But after Scott calmed down, he realized something very important: He didn't like to feel these things. Scott developed an understanding that if he wasn't responsible, he would feel things that were uncomfortable and potentially overwhelming. Through *experience* he learned that he didn't want to feel these things again, much a like a child who touches a hot stove and gets burned. The experience taught him that if he forgets his work again, his mom most likely wouldn't save him. What motivated him was the desire to avoid negative emotions.

Some would say that this would be a "shame based" incentive, but I disagree. The reality is that we want to teach our kids to be responsible and accountable for their choices. As much as we as parents seem very prepared to have kids experience the behavioral consequences of their actions (child spills milk, child cleans up), we tend to want to protect them from the *emotional consequences* of their actions. There are emotional consequences to actions as well, and it's important to allow kids to be accountable in this respect in addition to the behavioral consequences.

Third Outcome: Virtually all choices people make in life have a behavioral consequence. But people make many of their behavioral choices because they believe the outcome will align with what they want to feel emotionally. If kids don't understand negative emotions, then is there any decision that they can make that feels wrong? And this is, without question, the most important reason why kids should feel anxiety, guilt, and shame at young ages.

Think of it this way, when kids are potty trained, most of the time parents need to use an external reward as incentive for kids to use the toilet. At first, kids may get an M&M or something else as a reward for successfully completing the task. But, eventually, the reward goes away and kids are able to continue to display the desired behavior on their own. The reward is external (outside of themselves), but eventually kids *internalize* the feeling that the external reward generates and are then able to perform the behavior without the reward. They are now **internally motivated**.

Now let's apply the same thinking to adolescents. Pretend that they've either been protected from experiencing negative emotions, or told that the negative feelings that they have felt were the fault of others. They've never had to own negative emotions as their own. A situation occurs at school and these adolescents want to say disparaging things about a classmate for the entire class to see. So they decide to post awful comments on social media about this particular student. And they don't stop. Because they have no understanding of negative emotions, there is no **internal compass** to tell them to stop. To them, doing what they want, when they want, is the way life can and should work. After all, that's how they've been taught.

Scott's first experience with these negative emotions wasn't pleasant, but it was extremely valuable. While Helen and John may look at the short term compliance that Scott was fulfilling, the long-term value of him beginning to understand these complex emotions, and how they make him feel, was tremendously important. The situation generates outcomes on two levels. First, it generates the goal of compliance for Scott with regards to preparing for his school day. Second, it lays the foundation of feeling negative emotions so that he can be better informed in the future when he wants to make a choice. He now has ability to *foresee* the potential emotions he *will* feel after he makes this choice. This is the development of an internal compass and understanding of right and wrong.

All of this begs the question, if experiencing these emotions is so important for kids, why do so many parents protect their children from the experience?

My simple answer is this. Somewhere along the way, parents got uncomfortable watching their kids cry. It sounds harsh, but I believe it's true. Just like in the story when Helen and John tried everything they could to avoid a strong consequence for Scott, most parents do the same thing. They know there are limits to place on their kids, and they know that they should implement them. But they are fearful that the emotional impact on their kids will be harmful, and therefore many parents only set the limits that they are *comfortable* setting.

There is a belief that kids "can't handle" negative emotions. This is simply not true. It's the parents who can't handle watching them. The number of rationalizations that parents make to argue why some situations with their kids are "good enough" are unreal. I see it all the time. Parents want to make the status quo acceptable so they don't have to make choices that will create tension, conflict, and negative feelings with their kids, ***even though*** these things will better prepare their kids to be successful in the future. The justification for these feelings is filled with thought processes that rationalize why no conflict and happy environments are best.

This means that parents let poor behaviors slide out of fear of hurting their child's feelings. Parents inherently know that challenging their child is the right thing to do as a parent. But because they don't want to lose the positive relationship that they have with their child, they back off. Then the child continues to repeat the poor behavior and a parent can't do anything about it. Parents will lament about this in counseling. They will say things in session like, "I know we should have addressed this years ago, but we didn't want to make our child feel bad about himself." The idea that feeling negative feelings means feeling bad about oneself is 100 percent false. These are two separate things that parents must delineate from each other. A parent's job is to identify when their child is feeling something negative in the moment, while understanding that the negative feeling *in the moment* does not have to reflect how the child *constantly* feels about himself.

If a child feels shame about a behavior, it's important for a parent to identify the feeling, but reinforce the positives. Children learning the skill of opposite emotions being simultaneously true (otherwise known as ambivalence), is an essential life skill. But many parents don't teach it. They seem to believe that kids will learn about the negative emotions of life through platforms other than experience. This thought process doesn't make sense. How can kids learn about the emotions without feeling them? How can they manage the emotions later in life without having a sense of what they are like first?

We don't just pluck random young adults out of a crowd in order for them to immediately play for a professional baseball team. They play when they're kids, then high school, then college, then the three different levels of the minor leagues, and if they're lucky (and good), they'll play in the Major Leagues. This is the same rationale we should use when teaching our kids about emotions. They take simple math in kindergarten only to take algebra and calculus later. Yet we protect them when they are young from negative emotions, allow them to get hammered and overwhelmed by them in junior high school, with many becoming emotionally overloaded with pop culture shows like "13 Reasons Why" (a Netflix show that questionably validates suicide) in high school. Why are we surprised? We're the problem.

This leads to a larger question of what are parents so scared of? There is a crisis of confidence in parents to teach these skills to their kids.

As much as there is a value of teaching negative emotions such as anxiety, guilt, and shame to kids, there is a line that must not be crossed. In the story, Helen and John discussed and agreed upon an intervention that would lead to a negative experience for Scott that was just a natural consequence of his actions. They allowed for Scott to have the experience, coached him through it, and backed away.

If Helen and John took this as an opportunity to call Scott "stupid," "worthless," and other things that would make Scott question his value as a person, he would certainly feel shame and guilt, but it would not be positive. While no parent is perfect, communicating these things on an ongoing basis now makes kids internalize being "worthless" and that then does not lead to good things. There is a big difference between teaching kids the value of negative emotions and parents saying or doing things that force kids to internalize negative things about themselves. Please use common sense and don't disparage your kids and be punitive in the name of discipline.

Allowing kids to feel negative emotions will only help them be successful in the future. As parents, we desire for our kids to be independent and adaptive into adulthood. As parents, it is our job to give our kids as large of a taste of real life as possible. I've given presentations to thousands of parents over the years, and in my presentations, I ask, "Who here lives a completely wonderful, anxiety-free, worry-free, stress-free life?" I get laughter in response. So how is protecting our kids from experiencing real-life emotions going to benefit them in the future if we all know that life is chock-full of negative emotions?

We must be real. Life is hard and filled with many struggles. Our ability to respond in effective ways to these struggles is what makes people great. Kids will all have different fights to fight. But if they're not prepared to manage the negative emotions when these battles come, they're being set up to lose. As parents, we can't guarantee their success, but we can ensure that they are best prepared for the fight.

Chapter 3

The Entitlement Trap

The Story

"Great job Bobby! You are so smart!" Emily exclaimed.

"It was pretty easy mom," Bobby replied smugly.

Maybe it was, thought Emily. But her 10-year old son just put together a puzzle that he's had since he was eight or so, and was always just so impressed with the things that he could accomplish. She knew that there were many different philosophies on how to raise children. But she settled on an approach that she was most comfortable with: Reinforcing the positives and keeping negative experiences to a minimum. She believed that kids couldn't learn or perform well if they were experiencing negative things. Therefore, she focused on ensuring that Bobby had high self-esteem so he could thrive in a variety of environments as he got older.

"Bobby, can you please set the table for dinner?"

"Aww Mom, I don't want to. I want to go outside first."

"OK, just come in when I call you," Emily acquiesced.

As Emily was setting the table and waiting for her husband, Sam, to come home, she began thinking to herself that it seemed as though Bobby was getting his way a lot lately. She wasn't sure why this bothered her so much. It wasn't like he was acting like he always had to have his way, and he was helpful around the house. But school was starting in a few days and Emily couldn't help but wonder if Bobby would have some trouble entering fifth grade. Historically, he had always done well academically, though she had concerns about what would happen to him socially. She knew kids this age rarely had "best friends." Yet Bobby didn't express interest in getting together with anyone in his class.

Later that night, after Bobby was in bed, she spoke with Sam about her thoughts from earlier in the afternoon.

"Sam, why do you think Bobby doesn't talk about wanting to hang out with friends from school?"

"Who knows? He's a 10-year old boy without a great attention span. He'll focus on whatever is front of him at the time. I'm sure it's not a big deal," Sam replied.

"How can you be so sure? What if he is on the verge of having a major social problem? We can't just ignore it."

"He doesn't have social problems. Look at how he is with his cousins and kids on the block. He has no problems with them. Maybe he just doesn't know who he wants to be spending his time with yet."

"That can be true," Emily said. She hated that her husband could be so logical sometimes.

It was late and Emily let the topic drop. She knew she worried more than her husband did about their son, but she assumed that was the mom's job anyway. As she drifted to sleep, she told herself that she would reassure herself through what her husband had said, and see what would happen next.

The following evening, Bobby had a playoff game in his summer soccer league. He loved playing soccer and was actually pretty good. Not the best player on the team, the Phantoms, but certainly good enough to catch the attention of other parents. Sam wouldn't say it out loud, but he believed his son was the best player on the team. He did think that if Bobby had enough opportunities to play, he could really be great. Sam wanted Bobby to succeed more than he would like to admit, though he couldn't really put his finger on why. If asked directly, he would agree with the sentence that "winning isn't everything." But there was something inside him that would like to add on "it's the only thing" to the end of that phrase.

Sam and Emily enjoyed watching these games at least as much as Bobby liked playing in them. They would always share a good laugh with other parents at the games because Sam would always be yelling something at the players on the field, the referees, or Bobby's coaches. Even though in the moment his comments or tone of voice would be off-putting to parents, he was always able to laugh at himself and how he would get "carried away" in the moment of action. Bobby knew his dad was just another "enthusiastic parent," and didn't pay much attention to his dad during the game. The parents and coaches became familiar with Sam's behaviors and were always able to laugh it off as "Sam being Sam."

This game was no different.

"Hey Mike! Get to the front of the net!" Sam wished his work schedule would allow for him to coach, so he did his best from the parent sideline.

"C'mon, Ref! Open your eyes guys! Move your feet!" Sam was especially engaged tonight.

Bobby was playing defense and the game was tied 1-1. There wasn't a lot of time left, and Bobby's team needed to win the game in order to move on to the championship game.

As the opposing team won possession of the ball and began dribbling down the field, their midfielder crossed the ball into the penalty area directly in front of the Phantoms goal. It was a great pass and one that set up the opposing team to easily score and almost assuredly move on to the championship game.

Seemingly from out of nowhere, Bobby leapt in the air and intercepted the pass with his chest. Sam was silent. The ball was three feet in front of Bobby and a player on the other team was right there to take the shot at a wide open goal. Bobby quickly regained his balance, muscled his way through two players on the other team (knocking one to the ground), and kicked the ball out of bounds to safety.

"Great job Bobby!!" Sam screamed. "What a play! What... a... play! Absolutely outstanding! Couldn't have done it better!" Sam was loving the moment and hoped that the parents realized what a great player his son was. As he was watching the field, he noticed that rather than having the other team throw the ball in as the situation would suggest, the referee was asking for the ball. A player from the Phantoms picked it up and threw it to the ref. Sam was watching and hoping what he saw wasn't true. The ref was walking slowly to the marked spot on the field about 12 yards from the front of the Phantoms goal.

The opposing team was being awarded a penalty shot. From the sideline, all Sam could decipher was that the ref believed Bobby elbowed an opposing player in the face, causing him to fall, during the scrum for the loose ball.

"You have to be kidding me, ref! This is a big game! You can't make a call like that now!" Sam's tone had a sharp edge to it. He was really mad. This was a great opportunity for Bobby to showcase his talent in a big game. Now a part-time ref, with nothing better to do, was going to ruin his son's big moment. Sam wasn't going to let that happen.

"That's the worst call ever, Ref!" Sam was just getting started.

"Sam, please tone it down. I think you're going to far here," Emily didn't want Sam to embarrass himself or their son.

"REF, CLEAN YOUR GLASSES AND READ THE RULEBOOK! AWFUL CALL!" Sam wasn't letting up.

The referee blew the whistle and walked over to the sideline. From a distance, the parents couldn't hear what was said. Sam was appearing to be conciliatory to the referee, nodding his head and putting his hands out in a show of apology. But his face didn't look sorry. It was red and his jaw was tense. The ref walked back to the field to resume play.

Bobby was standing on the field watching his dad and the ref. He couldn't believe he just committed a penalty in this situation. It felt surreal as he never did anything wrong.

The ref blew the whistle again and the opposing team easily scored on the penalty shot to take the lead 2-1. The Phantoms didn't give up, but they just didn't have enough time left in the game to generate another good scoring chance and they lost the game 2-1. After the game, the Phantoms coaches gave the kids a nice pep talk and wished them a great remainder of the summer. One of the coaches pulled Bobby aside and let him know not to worry about the penalty.

"Look Bobby, I know you feel bad. But it's what happens in a game. From where I was standing, it looked like you got your elbow up and accidentally hit the other kid in the face. I know you didn't mean it. Bad timing at a bad spot in the game. But, hey, if you didn't get there in the first place, they would've easily scored. Your play gave us a chance. Keep your head up and don't worry about it," the coach encouraged him. "Thanks, Coach," was all Bobby could muster. He really appreciated what his coach said, but somehow it didn't make him feel any better.

As he walked to the sideline, he gave the requisite 'good game' comments to his teammates and nodded at other parents who said the same to him. Emily put her arm around him and Sam was silent. As they walked to the car, Sam broke the silence.

"Bobby, you made a great play but the ref made an awful call and blew it for you."

"I really thought I made that play. Coach said that my elbow came up and I accidentally hit the other player."

"Your coach doesn't know what he's talking about! You made a tough play. Soccer can be physical. That's what happened here. You made a clean play and had the call go against you!" Sam was evidently still riled.

"Sam, calm down," Emily was trying to slow him down.

"I'm still so angry about that call. Bobby really should've been able to save the game. Instead he was the victim of the worst call by that ref!" Sam really didn't want to let it go.

The car ride home was a combination of Sam recapping the amazing play Bobby made and how proud he was of him, offset by just as many comments that reflected the poor call the ref had made. "If only you didn't have that stupid ref, everyone would be talking about how great you are. That ref really ruined a good chance for you."

When they got home, Emily reminded Bobby of the chores that he still had to do. Bobby decided to put them off until after the game.

"Mom, I don't want to do them now!"

"But you said that before. And I let you put them off until now. I'm sorry, but you have to do them."

"MOM, that was the WORST game. I don't want to deal with anything right now. Can't I just do them tomorrow?"

Reluctantly, Emily agreed.

"Fine, but you have to do them tomorrow."

Emily felt bad about pressing Bobby to get his chores done after that game. She knew that he would be frustrated and would need some time to decompress about it all. The more she thought what she was asking of him, the worse she felt. Emily thought a nice surprise would be to do his chores for him. After all, they weren't complicated and he would certainly appreciate the fact that she did them for him after his rough game.

The next few weeks went by as usual. School started, and Emily was reading books about how she could help her son develop better social skills with kids in his classes. She also noticed that Bobby was getting increasingly emotionally reactive to things that would happen around the house. He would become easily frustrated if he didn't like what they were having for dinner, or would become upset if he had to get dressed up to go somewhere with his parents.

On one hand, Emily thought this was normal, as she figured most kids would get frustrated if they didn't like their dinner or have to put nice clothes on when they initially believed shorts and a t-shirt would suffice. But it just wasn't getting better and, one night at home, it came to a head.

"Bobby, can you please run down to the basement and make sure all the lights are off? I think we have to get you some new school supplies?" Emily asked harmlessly.

"WHAT?! You can go turn the lights off. I don't know why I have to. I haven't even been down there all day!" Bobby was mad.

"Why are you talking to me like this? I just want you to help me and please turn the lights off," Emily couldn't believe this was now an issue.

"I'm not turning them off and I don't care about my supplies! You can turn the lights off if you think we should go get supplies so badly!" Bobby yelled.

Emily was so frustrated. He needed that extra notebook for his math class. While his teacher said it was optional, she wanted him to be fully prepared for class. She negotiated with herself and told herself that it was okay if she went and turned the lights out, then took him to get supplies. She would talk with Bobby about his behavior when they arrived home from the errand.

"Bobby, what's wrong? Why do you continue to act in these ways? I mean, don't you think you overreacted even a little?" Emily was desperately hoping Bobby could see what she meant.

"I don't know what the big deal is, Mom. I didn't want to go. You always ask me to do things and I don't want to do them. You can't make me do anything I don't want to."

Emily feared Bobby was right. She couldn't make him. Now it seemed all this positive reinforcement she and Sam had been giving him was now becoming entitlement. Emily didn't know what do. She didn't want to talk to Sam about her experience with Bobby, as she thought he would just dismiss her. She also wasn't sure how to change her approach with Bobby. So she decided to keep the status quo. As long as she avoided conflict with Bobby, and tried to do everything on his terms, it should make it less tense at home.

And she was right. As long as she thought three steps ahead, she could head off almost all potential issues that would make Bobby extremely upset. Emily was frustrated at times that she had to do this, but it was better than experiencing the conflict at home.

Over the following weeks, that's how it went at home. Emily would try to sidestep all issues that may create conflict with Bobby, Sam would go on as usual (no sports for now), and Bobby seemed happy, although he kept to himself quite a bit. Then Emily got the call from school.

"Hi, is this Emily Johnson?" a voice asked.

"It is. Who is this?"

"This is Stacey Shelly. I'm the Assistant Principal here at Beach Elementary. Do you have a minute?"

"Yes, I do," Emily was nervous. She didn't know how well she was hiding it.

"Bobby had a conflict with another student today. They were in art class and apparently Bobby threw the other student's project in the garbage."

"Purposefully?? Bobby would never do that," said Emily defensively.

"It doesn't seem like it. But Bobby and the student started yelling at each other in class. It seems the other student was angry because Bobby wouldn't apologize for throwing out the project. The other student had been working on it for weeks and it was almost done. I'm sure you can understand his frustration Mrs. Johnson," Ms. Shelly said, hoping that Emily would take the hint.

"So the concern is that Bobby needs to apologize to the other student?" Emily got it.

"Yes. Please see if he can do that tonight. The conflict was substantial. We'd like to all move on in the morning," said Ms. Shelly.

"I'll speak with him when he gets home. Thanks for your call."

With that, they hung up. Emily was relieved that there weren't any larger issues that they needed to deal with, but still couldn't understand why this became such an issue at school.

When Bobby arrived home, she spoke with him about the call she had received.

"That is SUCH a lie!" Bobby was mad.

"What was a lie? Did you not throw out the project?" Emily asked.

"Well, I did. But that was only after that kid, John, was making fun of my shirt. He said something about how the color looked like it belonged on a girl! Then I threw his project out!"

"Okay, but did you try to fix the situation? It sounds like it all got out of hand."

"John said he was sorry, but I didn't believe him. You should have heard him. I wanted him to apologize again because I didn't think he was taking it seriously. He wouldn't, so I started yelling at him to apologize. He still owes me an apology."

Emily didn't know what to do. Clearly Bobby was provoked. She knew he wouldn't just do something like that. And she knew the frustration when someone would give her an insincere apology. It's difficult to invest in an apology of one's own after hearing that. She let the discussion end with Bobby for now, and told him that she would speak with his dad when he got home.

After dinner, Emily and Sam spoke further about the incident. Sam was in agreement with Emily that Bobby was provoked by this other student and shouldn't have to apologize to him.

"If anything, this other kid should have to apologize again to Bobby!" Sam couldn't believe it.

"That's what I was thinking. The school said they want Bobby to apologize. But I think doing that just makes it easier for them. What's right is for Bobby to get the apology that he deserves to hear," Emily had her mind made up.

"I agree," Sam confirmed.

The next morning, Emily called Ms. Shelly and expressed her point of view to her.

"I spoke with Bobby and my husband. We all agree that Bobby was provoked and received an insincere apology. If he had received a sincere apology to begin with, I think this whole incident could have been avoided."

"Mrs. Johnson, I don't think you understand the severity of the situation. It escalated so quickly. Regardless of what caused the situation to occur, its ending was so far out of line, that an apology is the only option that the other party and the school can accept to put this matter behind us," Ms. Shelly's voice changed and became more directive.

"I understand," said Emily, "but I just can't have my son apologize for something that wasn't completely his fault."

There was silence on the other end of the line.

"Hello?" Emily wondered if they had been disconnected.

"I guess the only solution is to have both sets of parents come in for a meeting since Bobby won't apologize. My assistant will email you days and times that work for me. Goodbye."

Emily was surprised about the abrupt ending to the phone call. Ms. Shelly seemed irritated. If she was irritated because Emily wouldn't simply do what she requested, that's fine. Emily's job wasn't to make Ms. Shelly's life easier, it was to advocate for her son. And judging from Ms. Shelly's tone, Emily was happy she advocated as strongly as she did. She didn't want her son pressured by adults in school to apologize for things that he wasn't responsible for.

Emily let Sam know what had transpired on the phone call, and he was in agreement with her. They had a meeting set up with Ms. Shelly and the parents of the other student (they found out his name was Scott) for two days from now. Emily was nervous for the meeting because Sam would be out of town on a business trip and couldn't attend with her. She knew he could be forceful, but nice, in communicating his point of view and she was hoping that she would be able to do the same.

When Emily arrived at school she met Joan, Scott's mom, and Ms. Shelly in Ms. Shelly's office. The office reminded her of the principal's office in the school when she was growing up. It surprised her that, outside of the computer, not much seemed to have changed.

"Thank you both for coming," Ms. Shelly said. "This issue between your boys has become out of hand and we need to resolve it. To make sure we're all on the same page, is it fair to say that Scott was making fun of Bobby's shirt, Bobby became enraged and threw Scott's project in the trash. Scott got mad but apologized. However, Bobby wouldn't apologize because he thought Scott wasn't being sincere?"

"That sounds right," both parents stated.

"Okay, then," Ms. Shelly was ready to press forward. "So how are we going to resolve this?"

"I think Bobby is owed a genuine apology. I think it's unfair that he is being attacked this way," Emily said first.

"Scott has apologized multiple times to Bobby, both at that moment and other times during the school day. Bobby won't listen to him and continues to say the situation was all Scott's fault."

"His apology must not be sincere then. We've taught Bobby to only to accept apologies when he believes those apologizing actually mean it." Emily was worried. She didn't know about the multiple attempts to apologize before.

"That's what makes this so concerning," Ms. Shelly interjected. "This situation should require a couple of apologies and then everyone should move on. I'm concerned because this is taking as much time and energy as it is."

"What exactly are you saying?" Emily was on to Ms. Shelly.

"I'm saying that Bobby is making this complicated. Scott wasn't perfect here, but he's been doing his best to own his role in the situation and to fix it. Bobby seems to think that he needs the perfect situation with the perfect apology in order to accept it. Forget this situation. If that's Bobby's expectation to resolve conflict, he's going to really struggle with relationships in the future."

She said it. Ms. Shelly said it. Emily was concerned about Bobby's social relationships and now she sees why. Emily and Sam had been so fixated on ensuring that Bobby felt great about himself, which was one thing. But they unknowingly also taught him to expect nothing less than perfection from others. That's why he had been struggling at home, and now, at school. He didn't know how to react when people wronged him and didn't know how to fix it. He also didn't know how to act when HE wronged someone else. Bobby couldn't handle not being perfect all the time.

Emily started to tear up in the meeting.

"Are you okay, Emily?" Ms. Shelly asked.

Emily nodded. "I'll be sure to speak with Bobby about apologizing to Scott. I'm so sorry, Joan, for this hassle. I appreciate your patience."

With that, the three women stood up, shook hands, and Emily was left to wonder what to do next.

The Lesson

"The Road to Hell is paved with good intentions," is a saying that can be traced as far back as Saint Bernard of Clairvaux (1091-1153). Similarly, when we parent our kids to always feel positively about themselves and to cultivate high self-esteem, we unwittingly create a hellish environment for them to live in. The damage that it causes kids is subtle and happens over a long period of time. When parents do finally become aware of what has happened, undoing the damage can be tremendously challenging.

Constantly reinforcing the positive, without the negative experience, paints a picture of life existing in a perfect vacuum for the child. Because of the way the environment at home works, they believe that all environments should reflect the same way. The reality is that the older they get, the environments will mirror home life less and less, rather than more. Therefore, the kids who grow up in these settings are at a tremendous disadvantage because they haven't been taught how to adapt and be successful in the real world. Seems pretty obvious. But if it's so obvious, why do so many parents fall into the trap of always positively reinforcing their kids?

Over the past 10 years or so, pop psychology made its way into the mainstream concluding that the better kids feel about themselves, the better they will perform in school, the more confident they will be socially, and the less likely they will be to engage in substance use or be sexually promiscuous. When kids have a strong sense of themselves, they are assertive and confident in most all other aspects of their lives. Culturally, we looked at the message and boiled it down to its most common denominator: Praise kids all the time. This oversimplification and clear lack of examination of its consequences is what has created a problem that exists in many towns and cities across the country: Entitled children.

Parents have repeatedly seen news reports or articles in magazines that state with a headline such as, "Confident kids perform better." They may not even read the whole article. They see the headline and say to themselves "I need to help my child feel good about themselves because then they'll feel confident." Parents don't begin to think that they can make their kids feel confident by helping them feel bad occasionally. One parent shares what they've read with the other, and a family dynamic is formed where empathy and support become the foundation and "accountability" is added to the list of four-letter swear words that shouldn't be uttered. As the child gets older, they first expect, then demand, empathy and support from everyone they meet and everywhere they go. The examples of how this has permeated our culture are plenty.

While this dynamic is already happening at home, we see it in our community when a child joins the local youth soccer league and quickly realizes that no one is keeping score (even though the kids know who wins and loses). Then at the end of the season, everyone gets a trophy.

The Buddy Bench

These kids may also go to school where there is "Buddy Bench." This is something that many schools put out in the playground area. The idea is that a child who is feeling lonely should go sit on this specific bench, which is the cue for all the kids on the playground that this specific student is feeling lonely and needs a "buddy." These other students should now approach the student on the bench and ask him or her to join them in their activity.

No one has been able to explain how this helps cultivate social skills for the kids who feel lonely. All it is training them to do is to act help-less and expect the world to save them. This does not breed confidence or assertiveness, it breeds passivity and entitlement. And the scary part is many parents and school personnel feel it's a good idea because they don't want children to feel lonely or isolated at school. While that is a noble cause, and the bench will provide a short-term solution, it does not provide a long term skill of learning how to independently form relationships. Adults have good intentions by investing in the short-term feel good, rather than the long-term skill building.

The Haves and Have Nots

After a child's experience with the Buddy Bench and the like, they move on to high school where it's a mash-up of academic and athletic competition, combined with empathy and support, the emotional Haves and Have Nots, if you will. The Haves are the ones that, somehow, through all the trophies and praise, were able to realize that they weren't perfect, and home life taught them humility. They are the ones that can effectively manage the athletic and academic competition by doing their best for themselves, not in comparison to others. They are the ones who pursue careers or trades they are interested in, and not the name of the college they want to attend. They can tolerate not being the smartest in the class, not being the most popular, etc. They can tolerate these things because they are secure in themselves. They learned to embrace the negatives about themselves, rather than ignore them and live only in a positive world.

The Have Nots are great in numbers and, in some districts, are a tremendous burden to the educational system. Schools are becoming centers of emotional support for this population of kids because they haven't learned how to cope with emotional stressors effectively by the time they entered high school. The Have Nots struggle with coping with stressors (many times having exaggerated responses to events, which in and of themselves are normal and expected for high school students). They demand nothing but the best of themselves academically, athletically, and with other interests, and can't tolerate it when they fall short of these expectations, which leads to high degrees of anxiety. They have a high demand for friends and social contact, either personally or through social media. They can't tolerate not being "liked" (either for real or virtually).

When overwhelmed, many students in this group increasingly turn to substances, self-injury, and, sadly, suicide, to manage their emotions. Limited school resources are now being used more and more for those who are experiencing mental health issues related to innocuous life events (such as earning a B on a test). Obviously, if a student has difficulty with anxiety or depression, they should receive help. But anxiety and depression to this level of intensity should not be caused by families who can't accept failure in their children, or who can't teach their kids to accept failure. This is sad and we should be calling more attention to this dynamic, rather than colluding with its existence.

The challenge is that the experience feels extremely real to the students who feel these emotions. The sad part is that no one taught them that many of their emotions are ones that all humans feel and, as a result, the students are unable to soothe themselves. They need to seek extra help to do so because their families didn't teach them the skill to do it themselves, nor did they identify and normalize these emotions in the first place.

Aversion to Anxiety and Accountability

Because of the message on the impact of confidence and positivity, parents seemed to develop a total aversion to watching their children cry. If kids cry when they get hurt, that's okay. But parents really don't want to watch their kids cry because of something that they can control. This means that children rarely experience consequences for their actions. Even the negative behaviors that children may display are perceived as "not that bad." A child may hit a sibling to get something they want. A parent may say "Don't do that" in stern voice, then move on. The child eventually learns that they can hit a sibling to get what they want because the parent may get a little frustrated, but there is no material consequence. A parent may get increasingly frustrated, but the child has already been desensitized to the frustration, and so the increased intensity in tone does not affect them. The only way to really have an impact is to have a material consequence such as a loss of privileges.

But too many parents have equated holding children accountable with crushing their self-esteem. That's not entirely fair. To restate: Too many parents are *fearful* that holding children accountable will crush their self-esteem. In fact, when I present to parents on this topic, many of them speak of feeling relief that holding their kids accountable is actually a good thing. They speak about being scared that they are harming their kids through discipline, and struggle to get the difference between a productive and effective natural consequence to a behavior and being punitive in order to generate shame in a child. By doing the former, parents can develop humility and empathy in their kids, which will only help them as they get older. By only being punitive, parents will work to make their child feel awful about themselves, and overall as a person, which contributes zero positive value to a child's well-being.

Anxiety that parents experience is transferred onto their kids. They want to protect their kids from the anxiety that they, as parents, experience. They believe the only way to do that is to make everything in the child's life GREAT. Again, a short-term solution. It's easy when kids are young. Parents can rationalize giving their children the extra snack or letting them watch the extra TV show. But as kids get older, it gets harder to meet those same demands. Kids want to go on trips, want cars, want, want, want. It doesn't stop and now external things can't soothe them nearly as well as they used to. This fear that parents experience is a tremendous motivator to make sure that their kids don't ever have to feel it. But that's impossible. Kids will feel anxiety, fear, sadness, or loneliness at some point in their life, and we must prepare them for it rather than help them avoid it.

Which inherently leads to a fact that most parents know and few want to admit: Kids are special to parents, but not to the world. I hate to say it, but it's true. It's the crux of why investing in a child's self-esteem solely through positivity doesn't work. There will come a time when the world will not treat the child as well as the parents do. It may come in college when they realize that the professors aren't checking in on them to make sure they are working to get their grades up. Or maybe on an internship, the children (now young adults) don't like the working hours managers give them. When they demand that the managers change the hours, they are subsequently terminated from the internship, blaming the managers for not being flexible. Or maybe it will come when they do obtain employment, but aren't given a raise because their bosses don't see them taking initiative to complete tasks. These now young adults are too scared to take risks and only want to follow directions they are given.

The examples are endless. But the outcomes are the same. Protecting kids from negative experiences or shortcomings about themselves will not help them grow as people and it certainly won't set them up for success into adulthood. Again, I'm not advocating for parents to be mean to their kids. I'm advocating for them to be real. Simple example: A child has a habit of interrupting a parent when the parent is engaged in a discussion with another adult. In the theme of the story, the parent would engage the child in the topic that they brought up, and then resume the discussion with the other adult, **every time.** Being real would be saying to the child any number of things in the moment, such as: "Can you please wait? I'm in the middle of a discussion right now." "Can you say 'excuse me?'" "Not right now. Wait until we leave." After this situation, there should be a discussion with the child about his or her behavior and the expectations the next time this situation arose. And then the parent must respond the same way again. That is being real and setting a child up for success.

In the story, at first glance, each incident in and of itself wouldn't be considered a huge deal that is detrimental to a child's emotional development. But as you can see, if the pattern of behaviors and expectations doesn't change, it can become extremely harmful to how a child perceives the world. Parents can make many excuses for themselves to in order to let the little things go. But if that's all they do, then there is no way the child will learn how to be responsible for themselves and cope with the anxiety and frustration they will inevitably face when they enter the adult world.

Parents must be relentless in communicating to their children what the expectations are. They must not be afraid to hold their children accountable to the natural consequences of their actions. By consistently setting clear expectations and holding their children to them, kids can learn how to display behaviors that will help them succeed and adapt well into adulthood. But most importantly, they will be practicing how to manage anxiety, frustration, and fear in ways that are effective to them. That skill will assist them in being able to not only cope with the hardships they will experience, but it will also not hinder their ability to find solutions to life's most challenging problems.

Chapter 4

Always Watching

The Story

"Jen...time to get up," Kate gently whispered.

"Jeeeennn," Kate whispered again, this time patting her daughter's arm.

"I don't want to," Jen mumbled as she rolled over.

"But if you don't, you'll miss the bus to school. Let's please get moving," Kate encouraged her daughter.

Kate had such mixed feelings about this routine. Jen was now 14 and a freshman in high school. Ever since elementary school, Kate had to come in and wake her daughter up in the morning. Neither of them ever discussed that this was something that needed to change. Now that Jen was 14, Kate didn't think it was worth addressing now. Her point of view was that now Jen was responsible for so much, she didn't need to be burdened with an alarm clock. Plus, Kate wanted to be sure that she did as much for her daughter as possible. Since Jen had started high school, it wasn't the time to set her up for failure. Kate wanted Jen to have every opportunity to get into a great college and achieve as much as she could.

"Come on, Jen. It really is time to get up. The bus will be here in 15 minutes and we have to be sure that you have some breakfast, too."

"I don't want to get up. Can't I just sleep in today? My English teacher is out today, and I have them first period. I won't be missing much. Please, Mom?"

"OK, if you're that tired, you can."

Kate knew Jen had a lot to do this year and didn't think sleeping in would hurt. Jen was tired and Kate had nowhere to be today. So it worked out for her to drive Jen to school. Kate's husband, Steve, didn't like how accommodating his wife seemed to be with Jen. But because he traveled so much for work, there wasn't much he could do about influencing the morning routines and concessions that his wife would make.

Kate looked at her watch: 6:30 a.m. She made a mental note to return to her daughter's room at 8:00 a.m. in order to be at school by 9:00 a.m. Kate sat at the kitchen table to sip on her morning coffee. She found herself wondering if Jen had turned in her social studies assignment about the first Continental Congress. Kate was very interested in the topic and helped Jen research the paper, as well as proofread it.

Returning to Jen's room at 8:00 a.m., she again tried to wake Jen up for school.

"Jen....Jen honey, time to get up."

"Noooo! It can't be time to go already," Jen was not happy.

"Yes it is, sweetie, let's get going, okay?"

"Fine, Mom!"

Jen threw her blankets off her as she swung her legs down to the floor and sat up in bed.

"Mom, can you bring me my sweatshirt that I left downstairs?"

"Sure, sweetie, just get ready!" Kate playfully responded.

"I will, I will."

Kate quickly walked downstairs to grab Jen's sweatshirt. While she was downstairs, she noticed one of Jen's favorite long sleeve shirts than she had left in the family room. Kate grabbed that as well to bring upstairs. Maybe Jen would want to wear that also.

Jen was ready to leave on time, and the ride to school was uneventful. Kate dropped her off and circled around to head home the way she had come. When she was halfway home, her phone rang.

"Mom! Mom!" It was Jen.

"What is it?! Calm down. Just, calm down." Kate sounded more under control than she felt.

"I forgot my homework that's due third period!!" Jen was in a panic.

"Okay, okay. Settle down. What do you need?" Kate calmed quickly.

"I left it on my desk! Can you please, please bring it to school for me? The grade on this is really important," Jen lobbied.

"Jen, I will. But you always seem to forget important assignments at home. One day, I won't be here to save you and you'll have to deal with the consequences," Kate said in a supportive yet stern tone.

"I know, Mom. I promise this won't happen again! Please bring it as soon as you can!"

And with that, there was silence on the other end of the line. Kate figured Jen had to get to class, so didn't dwell on her perception that her daughter hung up on her. Either way, Kate didn't have anywhere she had to be, so the extra trip to school wasn't a bother to her. She did believe that Jen would have to learn to remember these important items that she seemed to perpetually be leaving at home. But Kate didn't think that now would be a good time to teach her daughter this lesson as she clearly would be too overwhelmed to manage the situation appropriately.

Kate found a visitors parking spot directly outside the main entrance of the school, and headed to the office to leave Jen's assignment.

"Hi Kate!" the receptionist, Mandy, said from behind the desk.

"Oh, hello!" Kate was startled that she was already recognized by the staff at the school. "I'm just dropping off some homework that my daughter...."

"Jen, right?" Mandy guessed.

"Yes! You have a great memory! Yes, my daughter Jen forgot to bring it to school today. Can you be sure she gets it before her next class?"

"Sure will. Have a great day!"

Kate walked towards her car puzzled by the interaction she just had. Clearly, there was nothing wrong with it. The receptionist had been more than welcoming and helpful. But how did she know both Jen's name and her own? Kate didn't believe that Mandy would have ever seen them together. In fact, Kate had seen Mandy only when dropping off assignments for Jen. Could it be that Mandy only knew Jen's name because Kate had been there so often already?

Later that night, while Steve was traveling for business, Kate was reading a book and Jen was working on her homework beside her.

When Jen was finished, Kate wanted to gain a little more information about what happened that day at school.

"Jen, can I ask you a question?"

"Sure."

"If you had to guess, about how many kids have their parents bring their completed homework to home school because they forgot it at home?"

"Mom! What are you...making fun of me?! What is your problem!?"

"Jen, no, no. That's not what I meant."

"Well, it sure sounds like that's what you were trying to do. What, like, guilt me into remembering my things? I know I need to do that, Mom, and certainly don't need you laying guilt on me about it."

"Honey, no. That's not it at all. I'm asking because when I dropped off your homework at school, the receptionist recognized me and knew your name as well. The only way I ever see her is if I'm bringing your work to school. So I started wondering, if I'm there a lot and she recognizes me, are there other parents who come often as well to bring things that their kids forgot? And if so, does she know who those parents are also?"

"Oh, sure. I think every parent does it. You know my friend Tina, right? Her mom does all the time. Same with Sandra's mom."

"Wow, then that receptionist sure does see a lot of parents!"

"I guess so. I'm going to head to my room for a while."

Jen put her books away, rose from the chair, and walked upstairs. Kate thought about what her daughter had said, and it helped her feel better about her decisions. If other parents were bringing things to school to help their kids, then, of course, it wasn't a big deal that she did it as well. From Kate's perspective, all parents were fighting for the same thing: Their children's success. And they all knew that even the slightest misstep could derail massive opportunities for their children in the future. What parent wanted to take that risk?

Kate felt settled. She would continue to help her daughter in any way she could. Not only would her assistance only benefit Jen, it would also give her a sense of relief that she can help steer the process for her daughter, and ensure that everything went the way that it was supposed to.

The next few weeks went by as they usually did. Kate found herself enjoying waking her daughter up in the morning, and helping her out whenever she could. She made a couple of trips to school to help out, but nothing that Kate found intrusive to her life.

One Thursday, Jen came home from school and was tremendously upset. Kate knew she was upset because Jen was quiet (and she could tell that she had been crying).

"What's wrong, Jen?" Kate asked.

Jen sat silently.

"Jen, please tell me what's wrong. What happened today?"

Jen remained silent. She then reached for backpack and set it on her lap. She stared at it as if she were going to diffuse a bomb, but then decided to take the risk and unzip the bag. She pulled out a blue folder, and opened it. Jen stared at its contents, sighed, and carefully pulled out a small stack of papers that were stapled together.

As Kate was watching Jen go through this process with almost surgical precision, she could see through the papers that Jen was holding that there were many marks on them. Kate became fearful that her daughter had brought home her first C, and she wasn't handling it well. Kate had to quickly and mentally prepare herself to comfort her daughter and tell her that "everything would be okay." After all, Kate believed that while a C wasn't great, it was certainly a grade that Jen should be able to recover from with the right support and guidance, which Kate was more than confident in providing.

Jen slowly and tentatively handed the papers over to her mom. Kate confidently received them as she felt as though she was prepared to have the discussion with her daughter. Kate's eyes removed themselves from her daughter and focused on the papers that she had been handed. It was a math test, and in the top right corner of the first page were a number and a letter: 65, D.

Kate felt nauseous.

"Jen, how did this happen?"

"It's not my fault! The questions on this test are not even close to the ones in the chapter he had us study!"

"How much did you study for the test?"

"How much?! I knew everything in the chapter! We did the classwork in school and I always pretty much got everything right!"

"But did you study outside of class?" Kate pressed. While her daughter was clearly blindsided by the content on the test, she wanted to understand just how blindsided she was. If Jen really had studied and was having difficulties in school, she would need to look into getting a tutor for her. Jen couldn't afford to get these grades in her other classes also.

"I just told you, I knew it all! There was no point in studying at home!"

"Okay, okay. Can you tell me why the questions on the test didn't match what you studied?"

"Mom, listen. Our teacher said to us, if you can do the problems that I'm giving you now, you should be in good shape for the test."

"What does that mean?" Kate asked.

"He meant that if we could handle those problems, we should be able to do well on the test."

"Were the problems in class hard for you?"

"Some of them were. But I usually asked whoever was sitting next to me for some help, and they would tell me what I needed to know so I could finish the problem in class. I really wanted to finish in class because I didn't want to have to do it for homework."

"So, maybe you didn't know it all as much as you thought?" Kate was pushing.

"Mom! Don't you hear me? He said that if we could do the problems that he was giving us in class, that we should be able to do well on the test! I don't think our teacher was fair at all!" Jen was mad now. "It's like he wanted to set a few of us up to not do well! I think he enjoys creating misery for his students."

"Jen, how did other people in the class do?"

"Me, and like five other people, got either Ds or Fs. The rest got Cs or better. But I talked to the other kids who did poorly and we all said the same thing. We were doing well on the problems in class and thought we were all set for the test. Clearly we didn't think our teacher would make us all fail."

"Jen, I think there are two things here. First, clearly you thought that the test was going to be different than what it was. Second, honey, it sounds like maybe you didn't study as hard as you needed to in the first place?"

"Mom! I can't believe you're saying that! He told us we would be fine!"

"I know, I know. How about this: How would you feel if I reached out to your teacher to see if there was a way you could retake the test?"

"Yes. Please do that mom. What he did just wasn't fair." And with that, Jen stood up and went to her room.

Kate pulled out her daughter's math book and tried to compare some problems from the book to those on the test. Jen looked to be right. There just didn't seem to be any comparison between the problems in the book to the ones in the test. Seeing this helped Kate feel motivated to fight on her daughter's behalf. As it was Jen's freshman year of high school, she didn't need to be burdened with bad grades in the first semester. How would she ever regain her confidence in the second semester? Kate's motivation grew stronger. And the more she read through the test, the angrier she became. Kate could clearly see why Jen felt as though she had been misled.

When she had finished comparing all of the questions on the test to those in the book, Kate was ready for action. She picked up her laptop that was on the coffee table, opened it up, and went directly to her email to send a message to Jen's math teacher.

Subject: My Daughter's Test

Dear Mr. Newman,

My name is Kate West, and my daughter, Jen West, is in your fourth period math class. I'm writing you because she came home from school today with her math test, on which you gave her a D. I don't believe this is fair. Not only is it not a typical representation of the quality of work she is capable of producing, she felt misled about what problems would be on the test.

Because of this, I would like for you to give Jen an opportunity to retake the test. It's just not acceptable to tell a freshman what they need to know for a test, and then pull a "bait and switch" and put the completely opposite questions on a test. I'm sure you can appreciate my request. Please let me know when Jen can retake the test.

Thank you.
Kate

Kate read and reread her short email. She thought that she was polite and concise in her request and clicked the Send button.

Kate sighed and hoped that she would receive a response soon. Jen would certainly be anxious to know what her teacher would say.

There was no response that night, but when Kate awoke in the morning, she saw the following in her inbox:

Subject: RE: My Daughter's Test

Thank you for your email. Unfortunately, we do not allow students to take retests. I'm sure Jen is disappointed in her grade. She is always welcome to come in for extra help.

Please let me know if you need anything else.

Jeff Newman
9th grade Math Teacher

Kate was livid. How could she be dismissed so quickly? Of course, Jen was disappointed and, of course, she could come in for extra help! But he was missing the point! He should recognize how he misled her daughter and should allow her to try again because of his mistake. She decided to fire off a response immediately.

Subject: RE: RE: My Daughter's Test

Unfortunately I can't accept that response. I would like to meet with you as soon as possible to discuss.

Kate

Kate was so angry. She walked over to Jen's room to begin to wake her up, holding her phone so she could immediately see the response to her email when it came through. And it did about 10 minutes later.

Subject: RE: RE: RE: My Daughter's Test

We are available this afternoon at 1:00 p.m. Please confirm that you can meet at the school today.

Jeff Newman
9th Grade Math Teacher

Kate immediately replied that she would be there. She didn't let Jen know what was happening because she believed Jen would become very anxious about her mom speaking with the math teacher, and may even want Kate to back out of the meeting. That was not acceptable to Kate. She wanted to be sure her frustration was communicated clearly and wasn't going to leave until she obtained the answer that she was looking for. Kate was well aware that there were hundreds of kids in each grade and she had to be sure that they understood the importance of her daughter being treated fairly. The stakes were too high and being told the wrong things to study for a test was just not acceptable... especially if this test generates a bad grade that eventually keeps her out of the college she would like to attend.

Kate checked in with Mandy (who asked if she asked if she was dropping things off for Jen) to meet with Mr. Newman, and took a seat in the waiting area. She found herself getting nervous. As much as she knew she was doing right by her daughter by advocating for her in this way, she started to lose her confidence that she would get the outcome she desired.

A little after 1:00 p.m., Mr. Newman came out and introduced himself as Jeff. Kate introduced herself as well. They walked down the hallway of the school to a smaller meeting room where a third person was waiting.

"Hi Kate, my name is Mary Parker and I'm the Head of the Math Department," she said with her hand outstretched.

"Pleased to meet you. Thank you for taking the time," Kate nicely stated.

"Well, I wanted to have Mary join us because it sounds like you have concerns about the way the last test went for Jen," Jeff introduced the discussion.

"Yes. She didn't do well and firmly believes she was misled about what the test would be on. I believe her. And I'm here because, of all people, I think teachers should understand the pressures that students face, and should make accommodations should a teacher not give a student the correct information which then leads that student to bomb a test," Kate dove right in.

"If that were true, I would agree with you. But it's simply not the case," Jeff calmly stated.

"Did you not say that if the students could handle the problems in the class that they would be in "good shape" for the test?"

"I did, and I stand by that. But Jen was struggling. She didn't have a handle on the problems in class. I would see her asking the kids around her for help or answers. When I would come over to her and ask her if she had any questions, she would decline to ask any, and just turn in her completed assignment. While the assignments in class were completed correctly, she just didn't understand the concepts behind the problems. And that's why she performed so poorly on the test," Jeff stated his case clearly.

"So you let her take the test when you knew she wasn't ready?" Kate felt like she had an angle to play.

"It's not my job as her teacher to decide when she is ready to take a test. It's my job to teach and the students job to ask questions. If they can't speak up for themselves, how can they learn?"

"I can't believe you're not owning your part of this. So are you saying you're not going to allow Jen to retake the test?" Kate put it out there.

"No, we're not. The right time to have this discussion was two weeks ago when Jen didn't understand the material. I'm happy to help her, but she has to speak for herself."

Kate was feeling like she had failed her daughter. "This is disappointing. Mary, do you agree with this?"

"I do. Jeff is right. We want to help kids, but they have to ask the questions. And if I can make an observation, it seems while we are talking about how Jen needs to ask her own questions, I can't help but wonder why you're here asking these questions and Jen is not?"

That question made Kate feel like she was punched in the stomach. The air just got sucked right out of her. She looked at Mary and Jeff, but couldn't find the right words. Kate rose, took a deep breath to center herself, shook both of their hands, and left.

While she walked out of school, she thought about all of her choices in how she treated Jen. It was incredibly overwhelming to her. As she drove home, she continued to rationalize that she was only helping her daughter, and the teachers really didn't know what they were talking about. She then thought about what other administrators she could reach out to in order to fix this problem for her daughter.

The Lesson

Here we see what happens when parents' desire to help their child takes on life of its own. The empathy that parents feel towards their children turns into vicariously living through them. Parents will creep up to that line, eventually cross it, and then be miles past it when they start to realize that maybe they've gone too far.

The Danger of "Advocacy" and "Support"

In the story, Kate still feels like she's doing the right thing by advocating for Jen. That's the primary rationalization that parents make to remain hyper-involved in the lives of their children. They frame it to themselves through the lens of "advocacy" or "support." But while this perspective certainly helps parents justify their behaviors, it is incredibly destructive to the children. Let's put aside the parental behavior for a minute and focus solely on why the perspective is so harmful.

If parents view their child (who have not been identified as having special needs or other significant struggles by a professional or the school district) as needing to receive their "advocacy" or "support," then they also must believe that their child is not capable of speaking up for themselves. Because here's the thing: A child cannot, simultaneously, need the inherent advocacy and support from their parents and be completely assertive and confident. This is impossible. Therefore, the consequences of parents perceiving their child needing constant intervention are very harmful.

If a child is struggling to assert themselves in varying environments, the parents' role is not to "cover" for their child, meaning, parents should not simply do what the child cannot. It's an unsustainable practice. If they do, then the consequences that will occur will be very much like what happened in the story. The support will be virtually unnoticeable at young ages. But as the child gets older, it comes more to light, and the child becomes less and less adaptive and independent in their environment. This occurs because ultimately the parents were focused on the outcome of situations that arose, rather than the process of allowing their child to learn the skills that he or she would need to become successful into adulthood.

If parents coach and help their child navigate a situation, then the value is how well the child both learns and applies these lessons in various situations. The better they start applying these skills, the more independent they will become. But, in practicing to acquire these skills, they may be involved in many situations that don't go very well. And if that's the case, will parents be able to praise the efforts of their child rather than being frustrated that the desired outcome was not achieved?

The Vicious Cycle of Vicarious Living

This is where empathy eventually crosses the line to vicarious living. Many parents have so much empathy for their kids that they can't bear to watch them struggle. When that visceral desire is combined with the logical thought of "It's easier if I just do it for them," there is an extremely co-dependent dynamic created. The parent takes on more of the child's responsibility, and the child depends more on the parent for their own success.

As time goes by, the parent values themselves based on the outcome of their child's performance, which then becomes a vicious cycle. The parent is so invested in the child doing well because the parent's own self-esteem and ego is depending on the child succeeding. The parent is emotionally enmeshed with their child! But parents will continue to minimize its impact by stating that they are "helping" or rationalizing that their "child will grow up so fast," that they miss the point of their actions and the relationship that's been created.

When a relationship gets to this point, eventually it will have to break. As I stated earlier, a relationship dynamic such as this is effectively unsustainable. Either the child will want to break it, or the environment will. What I mean is that, eventually, a child will set a boundary with the parents, effectively telling them to "get out of my life," which will send the parents reeling.

Or if the now adult children will have to do something on their own, like a job interview, they may be so anxious about doing it themselves, that they'll need a parent with them. These adult children may also live as dependents on their parents and will most likely never move out to create a life of their own. If they do, it will be on the surface level only because they are drawing their emotional energy and validation from the co-dependent relationship that they have been so accustomed to having for such a long period of time.

All of this can happen because a parent doesn't want to watch a child struggle. Further, parents may over-identify to such an extent that the emotional enmeshment becomes catastrophic. And it all happens because the parents' perspective is that children can't do it on their own and the parents can't tolerate watching them learn.

Do It My Way

There is also a second scenario: A child is independent and assertive, but a parent thinks that the child doesn't do what they're supposed to correctly. The child is not handling things in the way the parent would prefer them to be handled. Therefore, the parent overcorrects the child in order to get the child's actions to match what they would do. When the child behaves independently, they will be corrected constantly, until the child gets the message that everything they do is wrong. At that point, the parent will begin to get involved because they can now fully control the child and their actions. Clearly, this dynamic is much more pathological than the first example, and much more devastating to the child.

Perceptions and Developing Assertiveness

Parents' perceptions of their child directly influence how they will act toward them. These perceptions, though, are just half the equation. The other half is how a parent will manage the emotions that these perceptions will elicit in themselves.

If a parent perceives their child as someone who struggles to be assertive, then a parent has some things they need to figure out for themselves. First, as a parent, how do they understand how to best help their child develop the skills necessary to become assertive? Some parents will argue that they must wait for their kids to mature through age and emotional development before they can learn that skill. Wrong! Kids can develop assertiveness at any age. It just depends on how invested parents are in teaching the skill to them.

Example: Parents know that they have a 10-year old child who is relatively passive. While the family is out running errands, the child states that they are thirsty.

There are two ways to address this situation. First, the parents, being concerned that their child is thirsty, will search for a place to either buy them a bottle of water, see if they can find a water fountain, or go to a restaurant nearby and see if they can pour water into a cup for their child.

Or, second, the parents knowing that their child is passive, coach their child on how to either buy a bottle of water themselves (while giving them a couple of dollars to do so), coach them on who to ask where they can find a water fountain (and how to ask), or coach them on how to ask a restaurant employee for a cup of water. By doing so, the parent is giving the child the skills to get what they need on their own, without the parent.

But here's the essential part of this second option. If the child does not try, and refuses to apply the guidance the parent has given them, then they do not get the water they are asking for. This principle is where most parents falter. It goes back to a point I made in an earlier chapter that parents don't like watching their children get upset. But here's a place where it's absolutely essential for the child to get upset. If the child doesn't try, why should they receive what they are asking for? As a broader question, in life, how many times do we get what we want by being passive?

As parents, we can look at this example in two ways: We can think about it purely in terms of the water, and therefore we will minimize the outcome because "It's just some water." Or we can look at it as an opportunity for our children to practice how to assert their own independence because we know that it will be essential for them to do this as they get older. We also know there are potentially severe personal and professional consequences when independence, assertiveness, and confidence are skills that are not fully developed come adulthood. Therefore, parents should hold the line if the child doesn't try to obtain what they are looking for on their own.

This may sound like a dramatic overstatement, but it's not. Let me ask you, if you don't push your child to develop assertiveness and confidence, who will? And if you don't push your child to develop these skills, how exactly do you believe they will learn them?

Just Like Riding a Bicycle

Parents have to get comfortable with the fact that in teaching their children to become independent, they will watch them struggle. While parents will not want to have to witness the struggle, they must come to terms with the feelings that they will have as they watch their child struggle.

Most commonly, many parents will speak about the guilt they feel if they see their child not achieving what they would like to. The parent knows that with a little intervention on their part, the child can now achieve what they need to and will be happy. While the logic is true and serves the needs of the parent in the short-term, it's entirely faulty and harmful when applied in a long-term view.

Here's what I mean: I would say 100 percent of parents I work with have a child who knows how to ride a bicycle. The child didn't learn how to ride a bike by the parent doing it for them. They had to fall a few times. They may have even become a little bloody and bruised. The parent, I'm sure, would comfort them, put a Band-Aid on the wound, and encourage them to climb back on the bike. The over-involved parent wants to intervene almost any way they can in their child's life to protect them from experiencing the inevitable emotional bruises that are coming.

So why exactly are so many parents scared of effectively doing the same thing with their kids when it comes to building the skills of assertiveness, confidence, and independence? Most parents don't feel guilty watching their child get injured when they fall off a bike as they are learning to ride it. Parents know that falling is a necessary part of the learning. Parents may not like to watch it, but they also know there's no avoiding hardship and pain when learning how to ride a bike.

Yet, when it comes to children learning independent skills, parents seem to expect there will be no bumps and bruises in this process. Why is that? They know that riding a bike (something that virtually every American kid learns) is hard. So shouldn't developing personal skills be challenging as well? This goes back to the point that, culturally, we have come to expect that the convenience and speed that many of our technological advances give us should somehow also speed the process of learning.

But learning is something that will continue to move forward at the same pace it always has, and the process won't change. Yes, there will be challenges, struggles, disappointments, sadness, and frustration. But through motivation, determination, and perseverance, there will be satisfaction for the learner. Many parents have lost trust in the learning process as they believe once their child experiences failure or discouragement, they will quit. And because parents don't want their child to quit, they will ensure their success so they never feel like they have to quit. It's a vicious cycle.

Parents, understand that you'll feel guilty coaching your child to be assertive and independent. It may at times feel really bad, in the moment. But take comfort in the fact that by putting them through these experiences at younger ages, you are setting them up to thrive into adulthood.

Chapter 5

Perfection Pressure

The Story

"Mom, where is my blue shirt?" Samantha gently called down the hall to her mom.

"How should I know? You're the one who put your clothes away!" Her mom, Claire, replied in the same way.

"But, Mom, I really need it for today!"

"I'm sure you do, but that doesn't help me find it! Keep looking in your room. It'll turn up I'm sure."

"You don't understand!" Samantha's voice was rising as she was walking down the hall from her room to her parents' room. "This is important! All the cool people are wearing blue today, and I have this great shirt I want to wear! If I can't find it, they'll all make fun of me! And if they do that, they may even leave me out of the group!" Samantha's eyes were filling with tears at the thought.

"Just because of a shirt?" Claire didn't get it. She wanted to, but the intensity and desperation that Samantha would bring to these types of situations made her focus on just finding a resolution.

"Mom! You don't understand! Just please help me find the shirt!"

Claire looked in all of Samantha's dresser drawers, in her closet, under her bed, in her sister's room, in her own room, in the laundry room, in all of the laundry hampers, and even the linen closet where the sheets and towels were stored.

No blue shirt. Claire was getting nervous.

"I'm going to be late for school! This can't be happening! Mom, I have to figure something out now!"

"Look, I know we can't find it, so why don't you wear that nice white, blue, and gray shirt you have? That should be close enough," Claire really thought she was being helpful.

"There is no way I can wear that! Are you kidding?! What am I going to do!?"

This is where Claire would get stuck. Her husband was downstairs helping their younger children get ready for school, and she knew he would struggle with this also. As much as they agreed that Samantha had to learn how to manage her anxiety when situations didn't go how she would like them to, her anxiety was almost always tied to real social consequences such as this one. On the one hand, Claire wanted to tell her daughter to "get over it," but on the other, didn't want her to experience a catastrophic social consequence just on principle. Claire was stuck.

"Well, since we can't find it, would you like to wear this one?" Claire held up one of her own blue shirts that she thought could appease Samantha enough to get her to school on time. Samantha looked like a young adult at 15, and could easily wear many of Claire's clothes.

"Argh! Fine! I guess I'll have to figure out how to make it work!" Samantha said with a caustic tone.

She took the shirt from Claire and escaped to her room to quickly finish getting ready for school. Claire didn't hear anything else, so she assumed that this plan would work for today. Samantha ran downstairs, grabbed some buttered toast that was left out on the counter, and was barely able to catch her bus for school.

"She can't go on like this," Claire said to her husband, James.

"I can't go on like this," he sarcastically replied.

Claire laughed. "She just struggles so much to be comfortable in her own skin. We've got to help her figure it out."

"I know, I know. But she's going to have to want to challenge herself in this area too. Otherwise, it'll get really ugly," James responded.

Later that night, Samantha approached Claire and apologized to her for the way she handled the issues with the shirt in the morning.

"I really am sorry, Mom. I just don't know what comes over me."

"It's okay. I really appreciate you apologizing for it all. But, if you could do this morning over again, what would you do differently?"

"Well, I wouldn't have yelled. I would have just asked. Instead of making you look all over the house, I would have accepted more quickly that it wasn't around and just asked to borrow something of yours."

"Makes sense to me. Why do you think you couldn't do it?" Claire felt there was an opportunity to explore a little more if Samantha understood what was driving her actions in the first place.

"I don't know. It's so hard trying to fit in with groups and I really don't want to mess this up," Samantha insightfully answered.

"But do you really think you're going to mess it up? Or do you just worry that you will, even though you know that you really won't mess anything up at all? There's a big difference between the two," Claire kept on.

"A little of both, I think. I really don't think I'm going to mess it up. But, I definitely wonder what would happen if I do? I just keep telling myself that as long as I do everything right, there's nothing to worry about."

"So today, as long as you had the blue shirt, you felt like you were doing everything right and therefore everything would be okay. You wouldn't be messing anything up." Claire said.

"Yes. That's why I just needed the shirt. I didn't have to worry once I had it, and that makes my day go so much smoother," Samantha continued.

"But, you seem to also understand that things would have probably been fine if you didn't have the shirt," Claire went for it.

"Maybe. They probably would've been, but I didn't want to risk it."

They hugged and Claire went downstairs to finish up some things before she went to bed. Claire thought about the discussion she had with Samantha. While she thought it provided some much-needed insight for her into how Samantha thinks about various situations, she also didn't quite know what to do from here. She heard her daughter challenge her own thinking, while at the same time not feel confident in her challenges. The only conclusion she heard from Samantha was that the only way to manage her fears is to make sure the external environment is exactly as the situation and context demands it so that she doesn't have to worry.

Claire spoke about this with her husband.

"Look," he said. "It's not that complicated. She wants everything to go perfectly so that she doesn't have to worry. But that's impossible. Nothing can ever go perfectly all of the time. When everyone seems ready, we're going to have to sit down with her and tell her that we just can't bail her out every time she feels nervous."

"I don't disagree with you," Claire responded. "But can we wait a little longer so we can get a handle on exactly what she's doing and why? If we jump in now, I worry that while we may solve the behavior problem she has, we won't help her resolve the anxiety that is causing it."

"Makes sense to me. How about we give it three weeks or so? Either way, we push for change. But I hope we'll have some more knowledge that will guide us in how to best do it," James agreed with Claire.

"Three weeks," Claire confirmed.

Of course, now that Claire and James had a plan, Samantha seemed to become more stable. The next week was void of any episode that was similar to what James and Claire called the "blue shirt fiasco." But Sunday night, as Samantha was getting her things together for school the next day, it happened.

"Oh my gosh! Mom, I need you to come here now!" Claire could hear the panic in Samantha's voice.

"What is it?" Claire asked calmly as she entered her daughter's room.

"All the girls are talking about how this new phone is coming out this week! It's supposed to be the best one for chatting with people, and I have to get it. Can you get in line for me at the store on Wednesday morning?" Samantha anxiously asked.

"Hold on, hold on. Are you serious? Phones are expensive. We can't just go out and get the newest and greatest thing because everyone is getting it. Are you sure all of these people are getting it?" Claire was totally perplexed.

"There's like 10 people who are having their parents get in line for them! I can't be one of the only people who don't have one! That'll be so embarrassing! Don't put me through that!" Samantha's voice was starting to quiver.

"But, honey, do you really think that people will make fun of you because you don't have a certain phone?" Claire was desperately trying to be clear.

"YES! I don't want to be put through this! I need you to do this for me! Don't make me have to explain to them why I don't have the new phone. Please, Mom?" Samantha's tone and face had the sound and look of fear coming through.

Claire again was stuck. She didn't know how to handle this.

"Let me talk to your dad," was all she could muster.

Claire knew James would not be game for this at all. They had another year before they could use the phone upgrade on their cell phone plan. Purchasing a phone at this point could cost anywhere from $700 to $1,000. There would be no talking to him about this. At the same time, Claire also didn't think spending that kind of money was a good idea. Further, she knew it wasn't going to solve anything. It would only be a temporary solution until the next issue arose.

The more Claire thought about it, she couldn't make this decision independently. Spending the money without telling James would be a bad thing. He would be pissed. But not spending the money and provoking her daughter's insecurities without telling him what she was doing would be a bad thing also.

While they were getting ready for bed that night, Claire broached the subject with him.

"So, I was talking with Samantha earlier. It sounds like there's a new phone coming out this week?"

"Yeah. Supposed to be a pretty big deal. Everything on it is bigger, clearer, faster, better than previous models. Sure will be reflected in the price, too," James always stayed up to speed with the newest technology. "I think they said if you don't have an upgrade, they're going to charge like $1,200 for it. Crazy, right?"

Claire didn't know what to say. "Wow. That is really expensive for a phone. Aren't they usually $700 or so without using the upgrade?" Claire was fishing for some information that would suggest that maybe James was wrong.

"Usually. But because of the new technology in this one, it'll be a lot more. I got the email from our phone carrier that they'll be charging $150 if you are eligible for an upgrade, but $1,200 if you're not." James wasn't wrong.

Claire stared at him.

"What is it?" He asked. James knew the poker game was over.

"Samantha said that all of these girls were having their parents get in line to get this phone on Wednesday morning. She really wants me to get it for her so she's not feeling left out," Claire was tip-toeing on thin ice.

"You're not suggesting...," James' voice trailed off.

"We talked about how we were going to give it three weeks before we made a decision. I know it's expensive. But we can't just rip the rug out from under her. She's so fragile right now," Claire outlined her case to her husband. She knew what was going to happen next.

"There is no way in hell we're spending $1,200 for a phone just because she's concerned about how her friends may treat her if she doesn't get it! This seems like a great opportunity for her to learn that if that's how her friends will treat her, then she needs new friends, not new phones. This is absolutely ridiculous. There is absolutely no way I'm even entertaining this idea!" James didn't know if he was more upset at Samantha for not being able to understand the significance of her request, or Claire for actually thinking about being on his daughter's side of the argument.

"James, can we just talk about this for a minute?"

"Talk about what?!" James held the line. "There is nothing to talk about. Even if we were multi-gazillionaires, there is no way I'd buy her something that expensive just because everyone else wanted it. No way!" James was clear as the vein in his neck started to bulge.

"I know. But hear me out. How will she handle this if we don't get it for her? Twelve hundred dollars is not a lot of money if it ensures she keeps her grades up and stays in a happy place with her friends," Claire was working to look at both sides of the argument.

"Until the next thing that keeps her happy costs $2,000. Then $4,000. When does it end?" James knew he was right and it was a matter of time until Claire agreed with him.

"Do you think she will be ok if we say no?" Claire asked.

That was fast, James thought. "I think she will be. But she's going to really struggle the first few days because she continues to look to things to help her feel secure. This is going to be the first time in her high school life where she won't have things to help her feel better".

"Let's go talk to her," Claire had come on the same page with her husband. She wished there was an easy way to do this, and she searched for one. But deep down, she knew this was the only way.

"WHAT?!!" Samantha looked like one of those toys that infants play with that, when squeezed, their eyes pop right out of their head.

"Sam, settle down and listen," Claire said calmly.

"HOW COULD YOU BOTH DO THIS TO ME?!"

"Sam, we're not doing anything. Please listen," James tried his hand at soothing his daughter.

"OF COURSE YOU'RE NOT DOING ANYTHING!"

"Samantha, we're going to leave for a few minutes. Once you calm down, we'll talk about this," Claire set the limit.

"HOW COULD YOU...."

Claire and James left the room, with James closing the door. They walked back to their room and sat on their bed for a minute in silence.

"Well, that went well," James sarcastically broke the silence.

"Gosh, I knew she would be upset, just not that upset," Claire said.

"Let's give her a minute. She's a smart kid. We have to reinforce to her that she can trust herself, and not these other things." James was planning for round two.

"I agree. I just hope she hears it."

They went back to her room, and Samantha was much calmer, although still had a look of fear on her face.

"Samantha, you're a great kid," James started. "Over the past few months, your mom and I have been watching you not trust yourself and instead start to believe that things are what people will value you for, not who you are. That's just no way to live."

Samantha stared at her dad. James took it as an invitation to continue.

"There's always going to be the next great thing that you're going to want. When people are in a position to need these things in order to feel accepted by others, they will eventually crumble because they just can't keep up with all of the new things. And the worst part is, these things have nothing to do with who you are. Just because you have this new phone doesn't mean people will like you. People will ultimately like you because you're caring, friendly, and empathic towards them. Not only because you have a phone."

The three of them sat in silence for what felt like an eternity.

Samantha was the first to speak.

"I get it, Dad, I really do. But you don't understand. If I don't get this phone, I think I'm going to lose my friends. I don't want that to happen."

"Then how good of friends are they?" Claire asked.

Samantha nodded.

"Can we give this a shot, then? Can we see what actually happens when you don't have a phone and everyone else does?" Claire asked.

Samantha nodded again. "I'm scared."

"We're here to help you. It'll be ok. It'll be hard at first, but you'll get through it," James said as he gave her a hug.

Samantha was clearly preoccupied the next few days, but wasn't talking about it. Other than a quick check-in question to her, they left Samantha alone with her fears. Wednesday morning she was especially agitated. Samantha was snapping at Claire, James, and her siblings in the morning. Her parents just tried to move forward without giving consequences, since they knew she was worried about what would happen at school that day. Claire and James just wanted her to get out the door and get to school.

After school later that afternoon, Samantha was clearly relieved. Claire decided to broach the topic first.

"Do I ask how school went today?"

Samantha smiled. "It was fine. A lot of those girls actually did get the phones. And they were really obnoxious to me that I didn't."

Claire was slightly confused. She expected for Samantha to be more upset if this is what happened. "So what did you do?"

"Well, at first I was really upset. I blamed you and Dad for making my life miserable. Then I started talking with a couple of these other girls who were being made fun of also. It turns out that I had more in common with them than the ones who got the phones. While I don't know them that well, I'm happy that you forced me down a different road."

"I'm really proud of you," James said. "You handled all of that really well. I hope you can see how it pays to be yourself."

"I do."

A few weeks later, Samantha had settled down with a new group of friends. She was much less anxious and seemed to be able to make more and more decisions based on what she wanted, rather than what she thought others wanted from her. Claire and James noticed this change and repeatedly commented to Samantha how proud they were of her choices and actions.

One Saturday night, Samantha told her parents that she was going over to one of her new friends' houses. She didn't tell her parents that they were meeting there in order to walk over to a party that another kid in their class was having at his house not too far from Samantha's friend. Samantha knew that there would be no adults there and a ton of kids were going to show up.

While at the party, it was the usual scene of some kids dancing, talking, or doing stupid things. At about 10:00 p.m., a girl from her new group of friends, Tory, pulled what appeared to be a clear water bottle out of her purse. It was actually filled with vodka. Tory said she got it from her parents' liquor cabinet. She'd had it a few times and said it made her feel "awesome."

Tory offered some to Samantha and three other girls who were standing there. The three other girls took a drink.

Samantha looked at Tory as she extended the "water bottle" to her to try. Samantha closed her eyes and thought for a minute. Samantha then turned, and walked outside to call her parents for a ride home.

The Lesson

Anxiety is the most common issue that mental health practitioners hear about from adolescent clients. Whether it's a primary or secondary issue, it is something that completely permeates the adolescent landscape. Anxiety is a funny thing. When under control, it is a tremendous asset to those who use it wisely. When it's out of control, it can be a debilitating illness. Current estimates indicate that about 40 million Americans are currently prescribed an anti-anxiety medication. So how can something that can be incredibly beneficial cause so many people harm?

The answer lies in the story. Many children are taught to read, write, perform math, or throw a baseball, while other children are able to pick up these skills naturally, without much effort or teaching. Emotions are the same way. Many children need to be taught how to manage their emotions so that they can grow to be adaptive and independent adults, while others can naturally pick it up.

But how many kids really learn how to read without help? Or write? Not many. The same holds true when it comes to kids learning about their emotions. Most kids can't learn how to manage them independently *and adaptively*. They must be taught. That's the crux of the story. How did Samantha's parents assist her to manage her anxiety when they saw that what she was doing to cope with it was unsustainable? And how did that process assist her to make a positive decision later?

Controlling Anxiety with Things

Anxiety is defined as a feeling of worry, nervousness, or unease, typically about an imminent event or something with an uncertain outcome. This is what Samantha was experiencing with much intensity and consistency, to the point that it was becoming overwhelming to her. Samantha learned that she could control her anxiety if she could control her environment by having the right things. In her view, if she didn't, she would lose friends, which had a high level of importance for her. Clearly, Samantha's desire to control her environment led to a thought pattern that made it next to impossible for her to consider other perspectives or potential outcomes to her situation. She was hyper-focused on things resolving her anxiety and the thought of not having them was unbearable.

Luckily for Samantha, she had parents who could see that her thought process was an unsustainable one. There was simply no way that she could continue to obtain things to make herself feel better. They decided that they needed to stop the thought pattern *even though they had the means to continue to provide the things* to their daughter. Using external items or outcomes as way to control anxiety is a dangerous proposition because it only temporarily resolves the issue until another issue takes its place.

Why Anxiety Over Good Grades is Bad

While for Samantha, the issue in the story was centered on items, in my practice we may see teens who struggle with anxiety about academic performance. They somehow tie their self-worth to grades and test scores. So they put immense pressure on themselves before each and every major academic challenge. They can't handle the emotions if they don't do well. These teens feel much anxiety before a test. They may vomit, have diarrhea, can't sleep, have obsessive thoughts, or other symptoms. It's only after the test is over and they receive their grade that, if it's a good one, they can settle back down. But only until the next test, and the entire process repeats itself.

Many parents can observe these patterns in their kids, but they don't know how to address the emotions, thoughts, and behaviors that their children are displaying. If kids are worried about grades, parents will think it's "good" for the children to be that anxious about their academic performance. Many times parents will reframe the child's anxiety as "drive" or "motivation," because it fits the parental narrative that the child must be successful in school. Therefore, parents miss the problem.

When a child's anxiety fits a parental narrative, parents don't work as hard to help their child because they believe that what the child is feeling is actually a good thing. It's like a parent that wants to stay in high social standing with an adult friend and consequently empathizes with her 8-year old child who says she needs a cell phone to talk to her friends. It fits the narrative. A parent will understand that anxiety and not want their child to experience it, so she'll give her a phone even though, for many reasons, it's not the correct social decision.

Learning to Deal with Anxiety

So how are parents supposed to teach their kids about anxiety? To begin, they need to not demonize it. I would argue that 10 percent of Americans are prescribed anti-anxiety medications not because they all need them, but because many don't want to feel, or can't handle feeling, anxiety. Of course anxiety disorders can be severe (Post Traumatic Stress and Obsessive-Compulsive Disorders to name two), but 40 million people don't suffer from major, severe, anxiety disorders.

Many people require medication because they have not been taught to feel anxious. Much of this is because of our culture, as I spoke about in Chapter I. Today, people don't get anxious about essentials of life because our culture has been simplified to where we expect food, a roof over our heads, and 250 channels on our TV. Two hundred years ago, people would become anxious about contracting the common cold because they may die from it. Our culture has evolved quite a bit, but we've lost the skill to manage anxiety in the process of this evolution.

Normalizing Anxiety

The first, most important, part of managing anxiety is to normalize it. This means that when a child experiences anxiety because of an impending event or likely worry, we should reinforce that the feeling is ok. Let's pretend a 10-year old has to give a short presentation to his class the next day at school. The child verbalizes his anxiety about speaking in front of the class because he's worried he'll do a bad job and the other kids will make fun of him. A parent might respond in one of the following ways:

"Don't worry about it. You'll be fine."

"You'll be great! Just ignore them. They don't know what they're talking about."

"Even adults get worried when they have to speak in front of a group. Remember to trust yourself. You'll do great."

I'm sure you can see the differences in the responses. And there's only one that acknowledges the reality of feeling anxious: The last one. Many adults believe that by acknowledging the negative feelings their children feel as accurate, it will somehow mean that their child will only feel the negative. Because of this, parents then respond with the total opposite reaction in order minimize and "squeeze out" the anxiety that the child feels. They believe that by not validating it, they are preparing their kids to cope with it better. But how can kids learn to cope with anxiety if it's not named or spoken about? The paradox is too great to ignore.

Sure, if parents use either of the first two responses, the child will be nervous and most likely give a good presentation to their class. But the kids are *teaching themselves* how to cope with anxiety. What if they teach themselves a maladaptive way of coping, like Samantha in the story? An extreme example of a maladaptive coping strategy is self-injury (cutting), which is all too prevalent in adolescents and an issue that I won't get into here. I bring it up because when parents can't teach their kids about emotions, kids eventually have to figure it out themselves. And they don't always get it right.

By acknowledging that anxiety exists, that it's common, and that it's manageable, parents are able to lay the groundwork to their kids that just because they are feeling something uncomfortable, it doesn't have to be a catastrophic experience for them. As kids get older, they continue to feel anxiety about a variety of things, but they are able to draw on the foundation of discussions with their caregivers that remind them that anxiety is normal, it's an emotion, and it doesn't have to control them. This then leads the now older children to feel confident despite their anxiety rather than being driven to eliminate their feeling of anxiety. They learn that anxiety will always have a presence in their lives and understanding it will only help them.

Which leads to the second step of managing anxiety called reality testing. It's a powerful way to challenge thoughts when kids are anxious. Reality testing simply means asking the question, "What's the worst that can happen?" In our imagination? Quite a bit. Let's go back to the example of the 10-year old who has to give the presentation. The fear and thought of a most likely outcome? That he'll perform poorly and other kids will make fun of him? Sounds bad.

But if we take that fear and break it up into three distinct possibilities, it doesn't sound that bad:

Best case scenario (in reality): Child will perform very well and be pleased with himself.

Worst case scenario (in reality): Child will not do as well as he'd like and have to "fight through" the presentation. But the other kids will not care all that much. They may even feel bad for him.

Most likely scenario (in reality): Child will do fairly well, and be relieved when it's over.

If we can challenge kids to consider that these three scenarios really are the most likely, suddenly their anxiety doesn't have to feel that powerful. It can help them learn that the overwhelming feeling of anxiety is just that, a feeling. It's not a predictor of a major impending failure that they are going to experience in their life. This then prepares children to put the emotion of anxiety in context. And that's the most important part of anxiety: How to use it appropriately in context of what is actually possible given the situation they are (or will be) in.

So now we can go back to the story and look at Samantha's decision making ability at the end of the story. The only reason Samantha was able to make this positive decision at the end of the story is because she was able resolve the anxiety that she was feeling at the beginning. She was fixated on ensuring that she had everything she needed to be included with her friends and not be ostracized from the group. Once she experienced the loss and picked herself up from the experience, Samantha realized that it wasn't that bad, and that the anxiety was scary, but not unmanageable.

If Samantha had retained the same thought process of being invested in relationships at all costs, she wouldn't have thought twice about taking the alcohol from her friend. Samantha would have been driven solely by her anxiety to not lose her friends, and this could have had severe consequences for her. But because she was able to realize that the consequences of challenging friends weren't as catastrophic as it felt they would be, she was able to challenge in the moment when the stakes were high.

This is the whole point of why it's important for children to understand and experience their emotions, rather than help them eliminate them. Kids are going to be placed in situations that can be potentially harmful. They will have one chance to make one correct decision, and they need to prepare for how they will manage their anxiety at that time. Samantha had already experienced a challenging social situation and relational loss. The practice of this hardship better prepared her to make a positive decision when a second group of friends pushed her in a direction in which she wasn't comfortable.

As parents, when we become fixated on our children only experiencing the positive because we want them to be "happy," we're missing out on the value of anxiety and all that it brings to kids. When kids can harness and understand their anxiety, they can't be deterred. They understand exactly what it is, an emotion, and they learn that emotions can create feelings that lead to inaccurate thoughts. Once they learn how to challenge their thoughts and bring them to a more logical conclusion, it is more difficult for them to be led astray. The kids that are in control of what they feel won't allow themselves to be swallowed up by fear and make a negative decision.

In the end, successful parenting is not only about helping kids perform well in school or belong to the "right" social group. Parenting is about teaching kids to make the correct major decisions in their lives in the moments that really count. Issues in school or with friends are just opportunities to practice for these moments. As parents, if we don't treat them this way, and instead treat school and friends like major life issues and decisions, we are not preparing our children to manage the real issues when they arise.

When those major decision points arise, we want our children, with all of the anxiety and fear that they may be experiencing, to think past the emotion and respond in a way that is assertive and independent for them, even if it creates more anxiety in the short term. Because if they instead respond in a way that will alleviate the anxiety and fear in the near term, they may be making a harmful decision that they can't fix later.

Chapter 6

The Illusion of Safety

The Story

"Come on! We have to go!" Angie was gently coaxing her 10-year old out the door to school.

"But, Mom, I don't want to go," her daughter, Carrie, whined. "Can't I just stay home?"

"I just let you do that the other day. I just can't let you do that again today."

"But, Mom! I really don't want to go! What if the teacher calls on me in math and I don't know the answer? I'm going to look stupid in front of the whole class!" Carrie was more whining than yelling in her negotiation.

"It'll be ok. You can do it," Angie encouraged.

"No, I can't! I'm too scared, Mom!"

Angie felt bad for Carrie. She knew that Carrie would be fixated on this if she forced her to go to school. At the same time, Angie believed that it would be okay if Carrie had the space she needed. Carrie would eventually "grow out of the phase" as she has heard many parents tell her. Angie also knew that if she could positively reinforce Carrie with enough good things that she could start thinking about herself, she would be more open to going to school and engaging in other things without the drama that currently ensues.

"How about this? How about I let you stay home for an extra hour, then go to school?" Angie proposed.

"Thank you, Mom!"

Carrie gave her mom a big hug, then ran to the basement to watch TV. Angie couldn't help but wonder if she made the right decision. As Angie thought about it, Carrie had always been a challenge. And not a challenge in the way the word was typically used when parents would describe their kids. Usually that meant that, behaviorally, the child just wouldn't listen or pay attention in the way that would be expected. Carrie was great at that. She was virtually always respectful, compliant, and generally easy to have around.

But that was also the struggle. It seemed Carrie wanted to always do what was simple and easy. Anything that would allow her to "fly under the radar" so to speak. Angie had been trying to get Carrie to be more active in after-school activities, church programs, and other social engagements with limited success. At age 10, Angie hoped Carrie would be more comfortable when surrounded by other children or in speaking with adults. But she just hadn't witnessed that level of comfort as of yet.

Angie also knew that her husband, Brian, struggled with how to manage their daughter as well. They both believed that children should be able to dictate their own interests and not be pushed into them by their parents. They believed that children knew best as far as what they wanted for themselves. Brian would agree that this way of thinking wasn't a problem through the first seven years of Carrie's life. But over the course of the past three, it has started to become problematic. Over the last three years, Carrie had shown that her interests have been in engaging in solitary activities, or being with her parents.

Both Brian and Angie have agreed that in and of itself, that isn't a problem. But the issue has been Carrie's sheer reluctance to engage in areas where there are multiple people present. This would include school and times where they would attend family gatherings. As the intensity of avoidance has grown in these other areas, Brian and Carrie became more concerned, but still leaned on their core belief that Carrie would eventually figure it out for herself.

While Angie was secure in her decision at this moment, and relieved to know that Brian would've done the same thing should he have been home, she was becoming concerned that maybe their interventions were not going to have the eventual effect that they hoped.

Later that night, after Carrie went to bed, Angie spoke with Brian about what happened that day.

"Well, we know she's not a big fan of school right now. It shouldn't be that big of a surprise that she didn't want to go. And it's good that you found the middle ground by not letting her stay home all day, and also not forcing her to go when she didn't want to either," Brian replied to the story Angie told him.

"I thought you'd agree with that," Angie responded.

"Well, I guess we hope that she does better tomorrow, right?"

"I would like to think so. I'm starting to wonder if maybe the way we're handling things isn't the best," Angie threw it out there.

"What do you mean?"

"Well, what if we're wrong? We thought that by giving her so much leeway and decision making power it would help her find her own way. But what if instead it's making it so that she's becoming scared of everything in front of her, and now she has no desire to go into uncomfortable situations? If that's the case, she'll never find her own way!" Angie was becoming upset at the thought.

"I think you're going a little too far with that. I mean, do you really think she'll never find her own way? Sure she gets nervous about different situations and they pose challenges for her at times, but Carrie may just be a 'late bloomer.' She may just want to be close to us. Isn't that a good thing? We should let her enjoy her childhood rather than force all of these uncomfortable situations on her now. There will be plenty of time for those as she gets older," Brian countered.

"Brian, I don't disagree with you. But what if that plan isn't best for her?"

"How could it not be? You see her when she's here. Carrie is happy, engaged, and fun. She just needs some time to figure out how to take those parts of her personality and show them when she's outside of the house," Brian was ready to wrap up this discussion.

"But what if she doesn't?"

"She will. We've always said, 'kids can figure it out.' They don't need adults always telling them what to do. Carrie's smart, she'll figure it out."

Angie felt relieved by this discussion with Brian and thought that he was right. Carrie was an energetic, likable, smart, 10-year old girl. Even though she wasn't moving along at the pace they each would like her to with regards to her social development outside of the home, they could see that she already had the skills to be successful.

That weekend, they went to a graduation party for Angie's niece. It was one of those parties that, as much as it was pitched as a graduation party (which it was since Angie's niece, Alexandra, did graduate high school), it was more of an excuse to have a family reunion. Angie and Brian prepared Carrie for all of the people that would be there: Aunts, uncles, and cousins that she either had never met before or had not seen in a long, long time. They prepared her with things to say, to be sure she looked family members in the eye, and answer questions with more than "yes," "no," "good," or "fine." Carrie was more than engaged in this, and she appeared like she was ready to meet with family members at the party. Angie and Brian felt good about it as well. They knew Carrie wouldn't naturally drift to acting this way with family, and they believed that preparing her the way that they did set her up for success.

As they pulled up in front of Aunt Karen's home, cars from other family members were parked so close together they almost stacked on top of each other.

"Is this all for the graduation party?" Carrie asked.

"Sure is! Look at all this family who wanted to come celebrate your cousin's graduation!" Angie tried to be enthusiastic about it.

Brian found a parking spot five houses down. He turned the car off, unlocked the doors, and both he and Angie exited the car.

Carrie stayed inside.

Brian opened Carrie's door and she was grasping onto her blankie (that she carried with her many places) and her seatbelt was still buckled.

"C'mon sweetie, time to go inside," Brian encouraged.

"I don't want to go," Carrie stated.

"But, Carrie, we have to. There are many family members here that we haven't seen in a long time. They're expecting us."

"But I don't want to."

"Listen, I know it's hard to see all of these new people, but you'll do great. You're such a nice, sweet kid. They'll all love you, and you'll have a great time," Brian was trying.

"I don't care. I don't want to go."

Brian sighed. He looked at Angie and closed the car door.

"So what do you think?" he asked Angie.

"What do you mean? She has to go in, Brian. This is my sister and Carrie is 10. She can't just avoid this too."

"How do you propose getting her out of the car then?" Brian felt an argument coming.

"Tell her that she has to go inside and that she'll lose privileges at home if she doesn't," Angie was set on this.

"Are you sure? We've never done that before. Can we just push her like that now?"

"We have to. Brian, it would be so embarrassing if our 10 year old daughter won't walk into a family party. Seriously, that would be totally ridiculous," Angie was scared.

She began thinking about all the times she let Carrie get away with not trying new foods, going to new places, or taking breaks from school. Angie really believed it was in Carrie's best interests to give her control over her environment. But now, as she was looking back, she could see all of the flaws in her perspective. Unfortunately, she knew that none of this insight would get her daughter out of the car.

Brian opened the car door, and Carrie squeezed her blankie even tighter.

"Carrie, we have to go inside now. This is something that 10-year olds do." He reached across her body to unbuckle her seatbelt and Carrie leaned over and bit his arm. Hard.

"Ooowww! Did you just bite me?!" Brian yelled as he rubbed his shoulder and felt his daughter's saliva in the process.

"I'm not going!" Carrie was holding the line.

Angie had watched this situation transpire long enough. She guided Brian aside and leaned into the car, "Carrie, if you don't get out of the car, and walk to this party like a normal human being, you will lose TV for a week."

Angie felt like she had regained control of the situation.

"I don't care! I'm not going inside!"

Angie slammed the door.

"Brian, this is ridiculous. We can't just allow her to dictate what we do!"

"I don't disagree, but we've been letting her dictate it for a long time. Maybe we shouldn't be so surprised that it's come to this."

Angie sighed. "So now what?"

"Well, we're here. I don't want to have a huge scene in the middle of the street. What if we give her one of our phones, lock the doors, crack the windows and we can go inside? She can text us if she needs to go to the bathroom or anything. Maybe after we're gone awhile, she'll want to come inside."

Angie didn't like the idea of leaving her daughter in the car, but also figured there wasn't another option. So she agreed.

As they walked inside, they spoke about the story they would tell to other family members about where Carrie was since they knew that would be the first question they would be fielding. As they walked up the front steps, they still had no plan and were on the verge of just winging the whole thing when Angie's phone rang. She looked down at her phone and the words "Brian Mobile" were on her screen.

Brian only heard Angie's side of the discussion.

"Everything okay, Carrie?"

"Okay, I know. Can I come get you and you can come inside with us?"

"Okay."

Angie hung up.

"Well she wants me to get her. She doesn't want to be by herself".

They both took the victory. Brian walked in and Angie went back to get Carrie. As the afternoon went on, while Carrie was quiet and tended to stay close to her mom, they could tell she was warming up to the other family members who were there. She began speaking in multiple sentences rather than just in one word answers and she did begin to smile more.

At the end of the long day, they all headed back to the car a little before midnight. Brian and Angie talked before going home that they would not speak about the events of the afternoon with Carrie. They just wanted it to leave it as a positive experience for her. As Brian entered the highway to drive home, he glanced in the rearview mirror and noticed that Carrie had already fallen asleep.

The next day was Sunday, and everyone was happy they could sleep in.

After attending a late church service, the family ran some errands, then headed home.

Carrie ran to the basement to play.

"So, should we talk about yesterday and what we're going to do from here?" Angie asked.

"Yup. You want to go first?"

"Yes. I don't know what to think. I hated setting limits that were so harsh about her losing TV, but that didn't even work. But then when we just walked away and let her experience being by herself, it was like she decided that wasn't worth it, so decided to go with us."

"Absolutely," Brian agreed. "It was like when she realized that she wasn't going to get her way, which may have been either of us staying with her or getting back in the car and going home, that she had to do something different."

"I have such mixed feelings about that! It's like we pushed her to choose between two bad choices! That's not fair to her."

"But when we give her two choices of one that she hates, like going to school, and one that she likes, like staying home, she always chooses the one that she likes. That's why she always wants to stay home. Not only does she want to, but we let her!" Brian was shifting his perspective.

"I know, I know. I don't know why I'm having such a hard time with this. So we have to clamp down a little bit. Is that what you're saying?"

"I think you know we have to."

Brian and Angie were huge Star Wars fans. They recalled the line in the first Star Wars (Episode IV, but it was the real first one to the true fans), when Obi-Wan Kenobi asks Luke Skywalker, "Who's the more foolish: The fool, or the fool who follows him?" Brian would use that line to remember that they should not be the ones following their daughter. They were the parents. They knew what the expectations of the world were, and they also knew that it was their job to prepare her for success.

So they made a plan.

Brian and Angie agreed that there would be no more days of Carrie being able to stay home from school. They agreed that of all the difficult behaviors that she displayed, this would be the most challenging to tackle. While they knew that they couldn't literally carry her to school if she was refusing to move, they could be more coercive and allow that leverage to work to their advantage as it did when they left her in the car for the graduation party.

Brian and Angie spoke with Carrie to prepare her for the change that was to occur at home. While Carrie nodded her understanding, this was uncomfortable for Angie. She just didn't think that pushing her daughter through threats and coercion was the right intervention for her as she knew how sensitive her daughter could be.

Just two days after their discussion, Carrie started testing. Brian left early for work, and Angie was still at home.

"Mom, I don't want to go to school today."

"Crap," Angie thought. "I don't know if I'm ready for this."

"Look, you have to. We talked about this. You can't just not do things you don't want to do."

"But mom, I don't want to go. Please, mom. Plleeease..."

Angie took a deep breath. She reminded herself that there will be situations in the future (like the graduation party) that her daughter will have to figure out how to engage in. She reminded herself that that allowing her daughter to not attend and avoid at her discretion was more of a disservice to her than a benefit. And she reminded herself that she and Brian agreed that this track was the best for their daughter. If she didn't implement the rules that they set forth, then that would also cause issues between them.

"I'm sorry Carrie, but you have to go to school. If you don't, you'll lose many privileges this week. What's your choice?"

The Lesson

Again, parents who mean to do well by their children somehow manage to mess things up. The avoidant child is another example of that. First, let me say again that parents do not like to make their kids upset. In the story, we can see that this avoidant child was actually primed to be made avoidant by her parents. Somewhere along the way, the child realized that she could push/manipulate (your choice) her parents to do what she wanted them to do. And she realized the more she pushed/manipulated, the more she could get what she wanted.

The Insecurity of Security

But let's pretend that there was a child behaving in the same way, only they really were paralyzed by fear in these situations. They really didn't want to engage at all and just wanted to be safe and secure by themselves. What would a parent do?

First, the expectations are the same, meaning that a child, through choice or fear, cannot expect to avoid challenging situations in adulthood. How many adults give work presentations that terrify them? Have difficult conversations with their significant others? Struggle to manage a situation with their parents or other family members? Adults can't avoid situations that are difficult. Giving kids the idea that somehow it is possible for them to accomplish this feat is a tremendous detriment to their ability to grow up to be adaptive and independent.

This is a point in many presentations I give to parents where someone would raise their hand (maybe) and say, "What?! How can I push my child when they're not ready?" It's not about making them a gregarious person when they are innately introverted. It's about how to ensure that the limits and expectations are consistently in place so they know what to do all of the time, no exceptions.

For example, many parents have a rule in their home that if you don't have a fever, you have to go to school. Why do many parents have this rule? To eliminate manipulation. They know their kids may try to fake stomachaches or other maladies in order to not go to school. But they also know there are times when they won't feel well, so the "fever" benchmark is used to cut down on the opportunities to be manipulated by the child.

Let's just expand that concept a little bit. Why is it ok to not go to school when the child knows they have an important test that day? Why is it ok to not talk at all to adults even when they are capable?

Why is it ok for them to use their anxiety to get out of something they don't want to do? And that's ultimately the trap many parents fall into. They see the anxiety and tears that their kids show and immediately empathize with their child. Parents will then protect them so the child can feel better.

But at this point, can we all agree that this intervention doesn't protect the child? All it does is (again) protect the parent. The child will eventually grow up, and along the way and into adulthood, will be directly involved in situations that they wish like hell they could get out of, but can't. It may be an argument with a significant other, or a disagreement with a boss, but they'll have to deal with it. As parents, we know this is coming. So why exactly wouldn't we prepare them for it? It's our job to prepare them.

Keeping Anxiety In Its Place

Anxiety is just a feeling. It's a worry and we all have it. The ones who are able to keep anxiety in its place are the ones who can adapt and function independently. Anxiety is something that gets us really thinking about "worst case scenarios." Kids have to learn what this feeling is, how they experience it, and how to best cope with it. Most kids when experiencing anxiety will just want to run away to somewhere that feels safe. The more we allow them to run and hide from their problems, the less able they are to cope with them. The greater the problems become, the less able the child or young adult is to cope with the problem, and the more they retreat. They are now caught in a vicious cycle. The problem is, in life, if retreating is the choice they make, they will experience a negative consequence because they didn't *deal* with their problem head-on.

It's up to parents to help their children deal with anxiety regardless of their drive to run away from it. It's not throwing kids into the fire (so to speak) to just deal with their struggles. It's a way of talking to them, and helping them understand what is happening, so they can be best prepared for managing their emotions effectively and then having their behaviors align. It's expected to feel anxious before a job interview, a big test, an important choice. But putting the anxiety in perspective and feeling control over it will only set up the individual for success in these events. Being overwhelmed by the anxiety can only ensure that the individual won't perform to their ability.

The Importance of Setting Boundaries and Natural Consequences

In the story, Brian and Angie created few boundaries for Carrie. They let her define what she wanted to do. That is a huge driver of anxiety in kids: Lack of boundaries. Kids just need to know the limits. When they understand limits and expectations, they actually feel more secure because they know what is and isn't expected of them. Without this, kids can quickly become overwhelmed because they can't decide what to do and want to retreat to avoid the decision altogether.

Brian and Angie didn't set boundaries, which led Carrie to dictate what she wanted. Only it became a problem when she was breaking the unspoken expectation that her parents had of her. This is where the work began for the parents. They had to start setting boundaries. And it's hard to do when kids are older. It's much easier when kids are younger to set limits, give consequences, and remain predictable because as those children age, it's all they know.

Children at 10 or 12 years old who start experiencing limits will struggle. They just haven't experienced the limits before and will push back. Hard. They want to be able to have control over their lives and they'll look at it all through a short-term lens of how it is affecting them today. The reality is that the parents should be looking at it through a short and long term point of view. Short-term is compliance, but long-term should be skill building in order to be successful later in life.

When parents have to engage in the fight about whether or not a child should go to school on a given morning, they have to remember that it's more than just school that day. While school that day may not seem too important, and a parent may want to acquiesce to the child, they have to remember that they are also setting the long-term expectation. In college, if their now adult child is tired or hungover, should she skip class? If he's at his first job and hates the project he's given, should he ignore it? Should he skip a shift at work if he doesn't want to go?

As parents, we shape our children's attitudes towards the world around them. The more we allow them to avoid what is hard, try to make their lives "smooth" or "easy," the more we are setting them up for failure in their personal and professional relationships as they get older.

The short sightedness of parents is what creates so many problems for parents. Again, they get caught in the thought process of what our culture says, or what the community expectations are, and simply can't make the best decisions for their kids. If a child is anxious about a class presentation and doesn't prepare, does a parent make him go to school to fail the task because of lack of preparation, or allow him to avoid it? All too many parents will allow the child to avoid the presentation due to the worry that the child faces about their poor grade, rather than face the natural consequence of their actions.

And natural consequences are an essential part of managing avoidant anxiety. Like in the story, by accident, Brian and Angie came across the natural consequence of allowing Carrie to remain in the car by herself if she didn't want to go into the party. Suddenly, Carrie realized this is not a consequence that she liked, so she made the adjustment.

Kids tend to learn pretty quickly, when their parents are consistent, that they'll have to deal with the natural consequences of their actions. And they learn that those consequences are most often worse than the task or event that they are working so hard to avoid in the first place. Once kids can learn this, it is easier for them to adapt to their environments and attain a level of confidence where they believe they can be successful in the areas where they once believed that they couldn't be.

A Special Gift from Adam Russo

Now that you have your copy of *Unwritten Rules: Real Strategies to Parent Your Child to Success,* you can now feel secure that there is more than just test scores that determine the success of your child. It is a great benefit to be reinforced that *WHO* a child is, not what they accomplish, still matters.

You'll also receive a special bonus I created to add to your toolkit. It is a special Bonus Chapter that highlights the struggles that exist for kids who have a desire to focus on STEM (Science, Technology, Engineering, and Math), and how to combat them.

There's so much confusing information out there about parenting. When you finish this book you'll be armed with what you need to know to see through the "noise" and focus on the issues that really matter to you, as the parent.

You can claim your special bonus for free here:

https://www.adamrussobooks.com/hiddenchapter

The sooner you know what the most important issues are for you, as the parent, to focus on with your child, the better your chances to raise your child into a successful adult.

I'm in your corner. Let me know if I can help further.

Best,

Adam Russo

Chapter 7

The Big Hoax

The Story

Brittney was staring at the SAT question and had no idea what to do.

27) $x^2 + y^2 - 6x + 8y = 144$

The equation of a circle in the xy-plane is shown above. What is the diameter of the circle?

She was lost. After taking the SAT two previous times with disappointing results, she was here a third time, and exponentially more perplexed than she had been in the past. She had worked so hard throughout school to get good grades, play sports, and volunteer. Now, with one question, she was feeling like a failure. Brittney wanted to be a journalism major, and didn't know what an xy-plane had to do with writing news stories anyway.

The road to this point was convoluted for her. It started before the first day of high school.

"Do you really think I can do it?" a then 14-year old Brittney asked her freshman guidance counselor.

"I don't see why not. You've been an excellent student throughout junior high school. So good, in fact, that it's easy to wonder if you're being challenged enough. As a freshman, it's a good opportunity to push yourself and see what you can handle," her counselor replied.

"But two honors classes her freshman year?" Brittney's mom, Mary, was skeptical. "With a new school, a lot more people and faces, it just seems like she's being set up to struggle." She turned to Brittney, "Don't get me wrong, I know you're really smart. But school is complicated, and I want you set up to do well in freshman year so you don't feel like you have to play 'catch up' for the rest of your time throughout high school."

Brittney nodded in understanding, but not necessarily agreement.

"Your mom has a point. I can see where she's coming from. But here's the thing to understand: It's your first semester of your freshman year. Even if you struggle, there's plenty of time to make a change where it won't affect your GPA too much. If, after a semester, you realize that it's too much work, we can always transition back to the regular classes. And if the grades aren't great, you have all of high school to make changes. Again, given your history in school, it seems like it's worth a shot," her counselor pushed.

Brittney looked at her mom. She did understand her mom's concerns, and she appreciated her mom not following the recommendations of her counselor blindly. But, she wasn't sure she agreed. While it certainly felt comforting to enter high school not being pushed in her classes, Brittney was competitive and didn't like the thought that she was quitting anything, especially before it got started. As her mom and the guidance counselor continued to debate the merits of starting high school in honors classes, Brittney had made up her mind.

"Mom, I understand what you're saying. But I think I want to give it a shot. Like my counselor is saying, if I mess up, I can drop second semester. I really don't think I'm going to mess up that bad. And, I'd like to see how well I can do."

"Are you sure?" Mary asked. "Once you're all set, there's no turning back until next semester."

Brittney nodded. "I'm sure, Mom."

"Well, then I guess we're all set," Mary stated.

That first semester, Brittney was happy that her counselor pushed her to take the two honors classes. They were hard, but nothing unmanageable. She also played soccer and volleyball, and was pleased with her ability to manage the increased workload on top of the demands of playing sports in high school. Her grades didn't suffer, and she ended the year with a 3.5 GPA. Her parents were also pleased with her ability to juggle all of the responsibilities she had. With school, athletics, friends, and occasional babysitting, her time was always occupied. Brittney was really feeling good at the end of her freshman year.

As the decision making time for sophomore year was approaching, Brittney was feeling confident. In her eyes (and her parents), she had easily exceeded all expectations in her freshman year, and her parents rewarded her by saying she can choose all of her classes (without objection) for her sophomore year. While Brittney thought that was pretty cool, she didn't think it was that big of a deal. For the most part, she thought, all of her classes would be the same. She'd just be able to choose an elective or two. Ideally, she was looking for some type of journalism class and was hoping to also find out about how to get involved in the school newspaper.

"Hi Brittney!" Her counselor greeted her. "What a great year you've had! Have a seat and let's look at your choices for next year."

"I would like to take some type of journalism class. Is that a possibility?"

"Yes, it is."

Brittney was thrilled.

"But there are a few other things we need to discuss. While you did well in your English and Math honors classes this year, I want to be sure that you would like to continue with them next year as well?"

"Absolutely. I was worried about how I thought I would do this year, but it wasn't too bad. I thought I was able to maintain good grades in those classes and still do well in my other ones. Plus, with sports, too, I didn't have much of a problem. That's why I'd like to get involved with newspaper next year also."

"Great, I thought you'd say that. But here's the thing. Your science teachers also believed that you performed wonderfully in their classes, and they are recommending you for honors there as well. What do you think?"

Brittney was shocked. While she had done well in science, she didn't view herself as a "science person." It certainly wasn't anything she wanted to do as an adult, and her interest was passive at best. Yet, she couldn't help be flattered by the suggestion that her teachers would suggest that she could excel in the class.

"Well, I don't know. It's just not something that I really want to do with my life. I'm glad they think I'm good at it and all, but I don't know if I really want to spend extra time doing work for a science honors class."

"I can get that. But here's the thing. You did phenomenally in science this year. If you go into an honors class, even though it's not your favorite thing to do, and get above a B, you would be setting yourself up for having three classes with weighted GPAs."

Brittney looked quizzically at her counselor; weighted GPAs? She didn't know what that meant.

"Don't tell me I didn't explain this. I'm so sorry. So, as you know, grades in classes are assigned a Grade Point Average, or GPA. An A is a 4.0, B 3.0, C 2.0, etc. If a student takes all regular classes, then the best they can do is a 4.0."

"Straight As," Brittney remarked, following her counselor.

"Correct. But, when a student takes honors classes, they are scored on a 5.0 scale. So an A is 5.0, etc. Since you have two honors classes already, your GPA is already over a 4.0 because of your fantastic grades. If you take another honors class, you can improve your maximum GPA and do even better in that area than you did this year. And, of course, after the SATs, colleges care the most about the Grade Point Averages of their students."

Brittney was sold. Even though she wasn't interested in science at all, she followed the logic about how taking the class could help her in the future when it came to applying to college. She had earned an A- in science this year. Even if she received a B in honors next year, her GPA would still improve.

"Makes sense. Let's do it," Brittney declared.

"Done," said her guidance counselor. "Now, let's explore your electives."

The rest of the meeting with her guidance counselor went well. Brittney was happy about her electives. She was able to get into an Intro to Journalism class. And the more she thought about it, she became more excited about the prospect of pushing up her GPA with the honors science class.

When she spoke with her parents about her decision, they appeared happy but concerned. They spoke about how proud they were of her to be recommended to another honors class, but questioned if she would be able to handle the workload of three honors classes plus a journalism class, especially when considering her school athletic schedule and now potential involvement with the school newspaper.

"Don't worry," Brittney told her parents. "I did great with everything I had going this year, there's no reason I should have a problem next year."

During the summer between her freshman and sophomore years, Brittney had volunteered at a local food pantry. She did want to volunteer to help people, and did see the value in her work. But she couldn't help but think that if she were able to volunteer a little more often and do it through high school, that the experience would look great on her college application.

The first semester of her sophomore year started off as she had planned. Brittney was managing her workload and other obligations with school and newspaper well. She couldn't help but look forward and anticipate what she thought her new GPA would be with her additional honors class. Everything was going wonderfully. Until it wasn't.

It started innocently enough. One Tuesday morning, at the beginning of her second semester, in her honors science class, they began a section on molecule construction and structure. Brittney thought it was hard. She was listening to the other kids in the class discuss the topic and ask questions, trying to learn from them, but she couldn't follow. They were going to spend three weeks on this topic, and she was already concerned about how she would do. Brittney took a deep breath and told herself that she'd need to get extra help for the first of two tests in the section.

Two classes later, Brittney's jaw dropped. In her honors English class, she was assigned to read *Wuthering Heights*. Not that she was against the author, but she really didn't have the patience to read about a dramatic love story for 450 pages. And she certainly didn't want to write an essay comparing and contrasting the two main characters, Catherine Earnshaw and Heathcliff, to Romeo and Juliet, who they read about earlier in the semester. She loved to read, but these stories about unrequited love were just... so... boring.

Her day ended on a high note when, in her journalism class, they were assigned to write a unique story about a topic they were interested in. It was completely open-ended, with the only requirement being that she had to interview two people and provide research supporting the history of her topic. Brittney thought this would be a fun project.

The next week was tough. No matter how hard she tried, even with extra help from her teacher, she couldn't get her mind wrapped around her science topic. Her book reading assignment was tediously boring. And she hadn't started on her journalism project. Plus, soccer was exhausting and she was on the verge of missing a deadline for the school newspaper.

At about midnight one Wednesday, her eyes began to well up with tears and her stomach began to hurt. She realized that, for the first time, she didn't think that she could keep up with her work. As much as she just wanted to quit, the fighter in her told her she had to press on. Brittney told herself that successful people didn't quit when things got hard, and she wasn't going to either. She took some deep breaths, wiped her eyes, and made a plan.

The next week was filled with deadlines. On Monday (in five days) would be her science test. On Wednesday (in seven days), both her journalism project and book report were due. She decided that she would devote the next two days to her journalism and English class, then the next two to science, and finish up with a refocus back to journalism and English.

Brittney worked harder than ever over the next five days. While she wouldn't define her situation as great, she did feel like it was manageable. When she walked into class on Monday morning to take her science test, she was surprised by what looked like some type of construction set on all of the desks in her class. The tentative relief swept over her. Was there not going to be a test today?

But then the bad news. After the students were seated, the teacher gave them their instructions for the test. And it was not a typical test. He told them to build a molecule, with all of the pieces on the desk representing different aspects of atoms. Brittney had studied the math and logic behind the molecules and compounds, but not the ACTUAL construction of them! She was defeated before she started. Feeling like a child in preschool, she did the best she could. Walking out of the class, she could feel the poor grade coming.

When Brittney arrived home, her mom asked if she would like to run out to the store with her as they hadn't done much together in some time.

"Are you serious, Mom!? I have a zillion things to do and don't have time to go out!" Brittney was over-reacting, and she knew it.

"Brittney, wow. Why are you talking to me like that? What's wrong?"

"Nothing is wrong! Why do you have to be on my case now? I have so much to do, just leave me alone!" This wasn't like Brittney to act this way, but she couldn't stop herself.

"Okay, okay. Maybe another time," Mary backed off. She gave her daughter a lot of leeway, and wouldn't typically let her get away with how she was acting, but decided that if Brittney was under a lot of stress, she would leave her be and see what happened.

Brittney quickly escaped to her room and lied down on her bed. She stared at the blank, white ceiling, thinking about how she totally blew her science test. She didn't want to even consider what the results of that test would do to her grade in the class, let alone her GPA. And she didn't have time to, as she had to spend the next two nights completing her journalism and English projects.

She got to work on *Wuthering Heights*. Brittney knew she wasn't invested and didn't care about any of the characters. But she did think she was able to complete some type of coherent paper that compared the characters so she could salvage some type of decent grade.

This didn't leave her much time to complete interviews and research for her journalism class. This angered her. While Brittney was most invested in completing this assignment, somehow she had the least of amount of time to do it. Her topic was "Teenage Driving: How Unsafe are Kids Today Compared to 20 years Ago." While she wished she could create a better title, it was the best she could do given the time constraints. Brittney was lucky enough to have scheduled an interview with the Drivers Ed teacher at school, plus a police officer the next afternoon. While she wished she had more time to put into the project, she thought she could come up with something good with the interviews.

The good news was that her science teacher wouldn't have the grades back to the class for a week. This provided a reprieve of sorts, but she knew it just postponed the inevitable. Brittney arrived home late after school because the Driver's Ed teacher was running late. She was able to complete her interview with the police officer and felt as though she had enough material for an interesting article.

Later that night, she had finished her article, and was starting to feel better about her workload. Even though it was a rough week, maybe she could recover. When reviewing the assignment one last time, she realized that she needed to incorporate research into her article.

"OH SHIT!" she thought. That feeling was back in the pit of her stomach. It was almost midnight, she was totally exhausted, and she needed to find research. Brittney quickly Googled "teenage driving accidents," and found some articles. She found some sentences that she thought would match the interviews and threw them into the paper.

"Good enough," she said aloud. "It'll have to work."

At the end of the school day, she felt relieved that she turned in all of her projects and could breathe. While she was not sure about what her grades would be, she was at least happy they were done. Brittney was surprised that she couldn't shake being bothered about not spending enough time on her journalism project. She knew she liked the class and the project, but didn't think this situation should be a big deal.

All high school kids have to sacrifice their areas of interest in order to complete the work in the rest of their classes. She had come to terms with that. And besides, it was more important to have the great GPA then pursue an interest. GPA is what gets students into the best schools so they can then pursue their interests from there. If they can't get into the best schools, then a student can't go far in the pursuit of their interest.

The following week started a downward, academic spiral for Brittney. She earned a D on her science test, a C- on her English paper, and a C on her journalism project. The grades were bad enough, but she also recognized that the weighted GPA would help her in this scenario. The teacher comments, however, really impacted her.

Science: "Brittney, I wished you would've come in for more help. It just doesn't seem like you have a handle on the material."

English: "Not your best work. While you made some good points, I wish you would've spent more time on exploring them. You can do better!"

Journalism: "Had the makings of a great article. If you spent more time on it, could've been an A. Try again next time!"

It was too late to change her classes, and there was more work to come. It was at this point that she regretted taking on the honors science class. Brittney hated science. If she didn't have that class, she would've had the time to excel in the other classes. Now she had to make due to with the poor grades here, plus deal with the classes for the rest of the semester.

Brittney fought through it. She worked incredibly hard but her grades suffered. She wound up with a C in science, a C in English, and a C+ in journalism. Brittney managed B+s in the remainder of her classes. But now her GPA for the semester was around a 3.0. At the end of the first semester, Brittney had decided she really wanted to gain entrance into Northwestern's prestigious school of journalism, and knew she needed at least a 3.6 GPA. Factoring in her second semester GPA, she was down to a 3.3. She had heard that Northwestern required a high score on the SATs as well. Her only hope was to get her GPA up in the first semester of junior year and do incredibly well on her SATs.

To plan for her junior year, Brittney's parents had a change of heart. They wanted her to remain in honors science. They thought she needed the help with her GPA, and if she wanted to go to a great school of journalism, they didn't believe dropping honors classes would look good on a college application. Brittney was confused and didn't know what to do. The pressure was immense and she felt there was only one right decision. She decided to go along with her parents, even though she didn't think it would be the best, since she was scared about the perception that a school would have of her if she dropped an honors class.

Brittney struggled out of the gate junior year. While it wasn't as bad as her previous semester, she wasn't seeing the gains in GPA as she had hoped. Because of this, she focused much of her energy preparing for the SATs. She needed to knock the test out of the park in order to even be considered for an elite university.

When studying for the SATs, she learned that elite universities, as a whole, require at least a 1270 on the test (with some variation). But, she thought that if should could at least obtain that score, she had a chance at some of them, even if they weren't Northwestern.

The first time she took the test she felt good, but ultimately scored an 1170. This was disappointing, and greatly concerned her. The second time she took it, Brittney was convinced she'd improved, and she did. To an 1180. The frustration mounted. Brittany had one last opportunity to prove she belonged in an elite group, to prove that her hard work, diligence, and motivation really mattered.

And that's when she found herself staring at the SAT question and had no idea what to do.

27) $x^2 + y^2 - 6x + 8y = 144$

The equation of a circle in the xy-plane is shown above. What is the diameter of the circle?

Brittney couldn't manage the pressure of the test. She was 22 minutes into the day long test and she had mentally checked out. She tried to answer the questions the best she could, but no matter what she did, she kept believing she was answering the question incorrectly.

During the reading comprehension portion of the test, her mind drifted. While she should have focused on the passage in front of her about an artist who lived in the 17th century in order to answer the questions immediately following, she began to think about how her life was going to be horrible because she was not going to obtain the score she wanted to on this test. She vacillated between being angry and extremely sad about her academic choices, questioning if all of the work was worth it.

After she completed the final portion of the SAT, she turned her answer key and booklet into the test monitor, smiled, and walked out. Brittney and her friends agreed that they would wait for each other once the test was completed to talk about how it went over some cold Frappuccinos, but she decided not to go. She couldn't bear to hear even one of her friends speak confidently about their own performance on this test.

Weeks went by, and she eventually did receive her score: 1150.

Brittney was heartbroken. She had no shot to get into an elite school. The opportunities that she was working for were disappearing right before her. If she couldn't get a great education from a school with prestige and a strong reputation, how would she get a job? Journalism was competitive. She needed to separate herself and she believed the school she attended was the best way to do that.

She began to wonder if she should switch career tracks. If she couldn't get into an elite school, how elite of a journalist could she ever be?

Over the weeks and months that followed, Brittney submitted applications to many different colleges and universities. As predicted, she was rejected from all of the elite schools. Yet, she was strangely comforted by the number of schools that did accept her; some even offered her significant scholarships.

When she received her sixth acceptance letter with a scholarship attached to it from a major state university, she began to wonder if maybe her experience would be for the best.

The Lesson

It's How You Go to School, Not Where

Brittney's story is all too common. It's a "middle of the road" scenario when it comes to high school students, academics, and applying for college. I consider it middle of the road because much of the academic pressure came from Brittney herself. Her mom, from the beginning, was not pushing honors classes, actually just the opposite. Brittney's drive for success was what created the culture of excellence for herself. It wasn't until her grades dropped that her parents became worried about what would happen to her ability to attend an elite school, and therefore wouldn't let her stop what she started. Many parents aren't able to hold off that long. The push from many parents starts at a young age, oftentimes earlier than freshman year.

Parents firmly believe that their child must have a successful future, and believe that the first step is entrance to an elite university. This is the first fallacy: While all parents should desire a successful future for their children, it is not dependent on entrance to an elite university. Recently, a study was published in the *Harvard Business Review* that examined what traits or experiences define a successful CEO. One of the conclusions was that "educational pedigree was not a predictor of success in the role," meaning that the caliber of school that a CEO attended was not a predictor of how that CEO would perform in their role. In their study, they noted that just as many CEOs attended elite schools as didn't attend college at all. Everyone else went to "standard" schools.

So the idea that an elite school can influence success is a misnomer. Frank Bruni, author of *Where You'll Go is Not Who You'll Be*, spoke about the concept that it's not "where you go to college, but how you go to college." Many parents and prospective students believe that the school will define them, but the opposite is true. **Students who maximize the school and its resources to their advantage will be most successful during their time there. It's how they go to school, not where.**

The Cultural Rules of Getting Into College

Here is a belief system that I've heard many parents speak about through my practice and speaking engagements: My child needs to get the best grades possible and be in as many honors classes as possible. If they do this well, it will set them up to be accepted to an elite school. Further, if they accomplish these things, it should also ensure a great score on the SAT or ACT. Once accepted to an elite school, my child can now have their pick of a career or spouse because they will have proved that they belong on an elite level. Once they graduate from this school, it will be easy for them to obtain employment because of their educational background. Once employed, they will easily "move up the ladder," make lots of money, and have no worries in their life.

Too many parents believe this. So many do, in fact, that it's one of the reasons that I decided to write this book! This belief system is incredibly harmful to our kids. But the strange part is that most parents will actually say that they don't believe it even when they just finished explaining why they do believe it. Parents know it's a fallacy and completely untrue. Parents will say things like, "I know I can't remove hardship from their lives, but I just want to be set up as best they can for adulthood." Or, "It doesn't really matter what school they get into, I just want them to do their best." But they can't stand by their own comments.

I have been in clinical sessions with high school students who have massive struggles with anxiety. Much of it relates to the academic pressures that they feel and their all-to-realistic fears that if they make just one mistake, they will blow their opportunity to attend an elite school, and thus ruin all opportunities for success into adulthood. Their parents will make one of the comments above, and when I push them to walk-the-walk by letting their child drop an honors class or two, or to take a break from a school club, they balk at it. Ultimately, as much as deep down they know that all of these things don't matter, they are terrified that they are wrong. Because of that, parents don't want to take the chance of ruining their kids' lives by taking their foot off the proverbial gas pedal, and therefore ruin their child's chance for success. So they continue to push not because they believe it, but because they are scared of not playing by the rules.

But what are these rules? They're culturally defined, most often by the communities in which we live. For example, communities of high socioeconomic class and means define these rules rigidly, yet they are unwritten. The communities are wealthy and typically have many residents who have been able to obtain some significant measure of success in their lives. This in turn leads to a push to have their kids exceed the success that the parents have achieved. But being at an already high level, it is more difficult to achieve.

Parents will learn though social media or small talk with other parents that so-and-so enrolled their child in the premier SAT prep class, or signed up their child for the extra honors class. The tone of the parent who enrolled their child in these classes is, "I'm a step ahead of you," and the parent who is listening has a reaction of, "Shit, I'm behind." Then that parent goes into a panic about what they need to do for their child to allow them to keep up with what they now perceive "everyone" is doing. In the end, it's the kids who are eventually squeezed and suffer. But the parents don't seem to care because they are operating in the best interests of their kids, and don't seem to mind that there are, at times, catastrophic consequences. So parents push, thinking they are doing the best they can.

And these cultures are replicated across the country. I would argue that affluent, suburban, family-driven towns on the outskirts of major cities across the country struggle with the exact same issue. The high socioeconomic standing pushes parents to push their kids harder.

Success Without Hardship?

While parents desire success for their children, they don't actually talk about what they really mean. The statement "I desire success for my children" is three-quarters of what they mean. The real statement that many parents believe is "I desire success for my child, without hardship." It's that last part that causes all of the stress at home, starting in high school. There is no possible way to avoid hardship when it comes to pursuing success. And this is a major part of how our culture influences the college process. Culture tells us that everything should be happening quickly and easily. But that's not how life works, especially when it comes to college and then professional careers. Yet somehow more and more parents are expecting it.

But parents' commitment to this belief is totally arbitrary. For example, let's say a parent works for a large company in a human resources position in charge of hiring. This parent receives a resume from a young man who is a recent grad at a state school. The cover letter and experience show that this young adult, through perseverance and determination, was able to attend college despite growing up in a challenging (and at times devastating) inner city environment. That parent/human resources person would believe that potential employee had promise because of his experience and would most likely (if everything else looked like a fit) grant him at least an interview.

Yet that same parent would believe those experiences wouldn't apply to his own children. In fact, they actually prevent his children from even having those experiences! Many parents in these communities believe that it is their sole responsibility to protect their children from hardships (i.e., anxiety, pressure, sadness, disappointment, etc.) so that their children can be successful.

Do you see the irony yet? Parents in their personal lives would protect their child from experiencing hardships that they would, in turn, value in their professional lives. It doesn't make sense. Yet parents perpetuate this over and over again. They don't want their kids to make mistakes or have struggles, let alone be able to learn from them. For many parents, mistakes and struggles are seen as getting in the way of achieving the eventual success they believe their children should attain.

A Better Predictor of Future Earnings?

Sadly, kids are the ones who are always caught in the middle. They hear information from their local school districts and their parents telling them that they need certain GPAs and standardized test scores to be admitted to elite colleges. At home, attending any other educational institution (other than an elite one) is often considered to be a failure and a disappointment to the parents. So kids feel like they have no choice. They push themselves even though the anxiety and panic may become incredibly difficult to bear. Parents will put their kids on medication and take them to counseling to help them cope. But they don't want to consider the possibility that pulling out of the race would be the best thing for their child. Parents can't handle that type of disappointment.

But again, there are countless studies that state that these things that our cultural bubbles define as important—GPA, SAT score, college attended—are not relevant to future success. My favorite study is one that was done between Princeton University and the Mathematica Institute in 2011. It set out to explore how much more money, over the course of a lifetime, could be expected to be earned by those who graduated from elite universities (Ivy League, Duke, Stanford, etc.) when compared to non-elite universities (everywhere else). What the researchers concluded was that:

"The better predictor of future earnings was the average SAT scores of the schools that a student applied to and not the average SAT scores of the schools they actually attend."

Let that sink in. The best predictor of future earnings was the average SAT scores of the **schools that a student applied to** and **not the average scores of the schools that they actually attend.** That doesn't make any sense. Shouldn't the scores of the schools they attend affect their earnings more than the ones they apply to? No, say the researchers. They concluded that in the end, it was the motivation and determination of the applicants that determined their success in the future, and not the school they attended.

This is a relative study. It doesn't mean every teenager, regardless of SAT scores, should just apply to an elite school. It means that if a student has an outside chance, and wants to push to get into a school that requires better than what their numbers (GPA, SAT) would suggest, the trait of having the motivation to push themselves is a greater predictor of success than just attending whatever college they perceive to be the "safest" for them.

The results of this study fly in the face of what culture says about college. Culture says that only students who attend the best schools can make the best living. Malcolm Gladwell in his book, *David and Goliath*, spoke about this issue as well. In his chapter, "Big Fish Small Pond," he concluded (in summary of much research) that students should attend schools that aren't elite, because when a college student can perceive themselves as being one of the smartest in a class, the quality of their work and outcomes will be good. When a student perceives himself to be one of the dumbest in a class, they will struggle and quit. Hence, this is why, statistically, it's better to be the smartest person in a "non-elite" educational institution, rather than being barely qualifying and being accepted to an "elite" college.

The Problem of College Perception

But here's where I have a problem. If motivation and determination are typically deciding factors for success of students, why should we look to place them in an environment that doesn't challenge them? I believe Malcom Gladwell's conclusions are culturally manufactured as well. They are a way to quantify how to have kids obtain the best outcomes with the least amount of pressure. I would want to know why we're not better preparing our kids for the struggle that they'll face in college, rather than show them data that validates why they should avoid the pressure in the first place in order to achieve success.

Which leads to the crux of why all of the college perception is problematic:

Our culture simply does not value the educational process. The culture only values the outcomes.

Parents are invested in the outcomes, and they miss the point of the value of the process kids experience to achieve it. Parents focus on questions like "What's your grade?" or "How'd you do on the test?", and don't spend enough time on questions like "How hard did you study?" or "How come that class is hard?" In the cultural bubble, we believe that outcomes are all that matter because they are the answer to life's hardships. But, the value of the process is actually more revered than the outcomes themselves.

I would argue that a student who earns a C on a test gets extra help and studies hard only to get a B on the next test, has learned more than the student who didn't have to study to get a B+ on the same test. The process is what is important. The process says it's impossible to know everything one needs to immediately, yet our educational culture says that we should. Because our culture is scared, somewhere along the way it stopped trusting the process and became more focused on outcomes. And this outcome driven culture has driven too many high school students towards substance use and suicide while chasing the unattainable goal of perfection.

From the study published in the *Harvard Business Review* looking at traits and experiences of a successful CEO, of the CEO candidates reviewed, 45 percent of them had a ***major professional catastrophe occur prior to obtaining*** the lead role of Chief Executive Officer. These catastrophes ranged from job loss to decisions that cost their companies millions of dollars. But they were able to learn from and overcome these experiences in order to reach the top of the ladder. Seventy-eight percent of this subgroup did eventually go on to become a CEO. The study directly refutes what most people believe: That people in a CEO role have had a nice, steady, consistent, trend line up the corporate ladder to the top.

Our investment in outcomes makes us miss the point of learning from the failures that will inevitably occur. The setbacks that kids experience in school, whether academic, social, or otherwise, help them develop as a person. Our failures as parents occur when we don't take the opportunity to coach them through these experiences, and instead hammer them about their failure to achieve the consequence. When we don't allow kids to learn from their academic failures, we're not allowing them to learn about their interests and themselves.

If parents really want their kids to be successful, they will allow them to explore their interests and then give them the freedom to be successful in those areas. Instead, we have taken a perspective that all kids have to perform at the highest academic levels in all classes, all the time. Because if they don't, they will experience a significant consequence when it comes to applying for college.

Our cultural bubbles miss the point. While we are focusing on outcomes and competing with our neighbors in order to get the edge in the "elite college admissions race," we're doing a disservice to our kids. Rather than focusing our energy on areas that can't be won, we should be focusing on developing our kids personally. **Push them, yes, but push *them* to do *their* best, not because they're not achieving the outcome *you* want.** Let our kids learn, challenge themselves, develop new interests, and have fun. The things that we believe matter actually don't.

When I give presentations, I always ask parents when was the last time someone asked them what college they attended. I asked them if they know where their boss or colleagues attended. If they didn't attend Ohio State or Michigan (big football rivalry in the Midwest), most people didn't know. And that's the point. **No one cares what school you went to or what your SAT scores are.**

Business values *who* you are, not *what* you've done. As parents, we have a finite opportunity to shape this in our kids. Let's not spoil it by focusing on all of the wrong things that don't matter to their future. Focus on what does: Who they are, their principles, values, and morals. If these are developed correctly, it will be a greater predictor to their future success than any SAT score ever will be.

Chapter 8

The College Setup

The Story

"This isn't that bad," Grant thought. He held the stack of papers in his hands and was slowly flipping through them, page by page. Everyone always said that college would be hard. But as he was examining the syllabi for the first five classes of his freshman year, he started to relax.

He had just been admitted to a reputable school that was about a five-hour drive from home—far enough where his parents couldn't visit him every weekend (and vice versa), but close enough that if he needed anything he could always go.

Grant had performed well in high school. He was an athlete, achieved high grades, and over-performed on his SATs. He didn't know what he wanted to do professionally as of yet, but he figured he had some time to figure it out.

His parents left two days earlier after helping him get settled in his dorm room. Grant had a roommate, Jon, who lived really far away. While they spoke a little bit, it was clear from the outset that they were going to travel in different circles. Grant was going to pursue something in the business/finance world, while Jon was going into medicine. He hoped to be able to get along with his roommate his freshman year. But judging from the courses that Jon had to take, he wouldn't be seeing much of him as he had a lot of studying to do.

Jon had left to go to a pre-med orientation for the afternoon and the dorm was pretty quiet. Students still had a few days to check in and many still had not arrived. In the orientation packet Grant received, he was given the syllabi for his classes.

The workload didn't look too bad. Seemed like a few tests and final for each class. Some classes had papers to write as well. But for the most part, it actually looked easier than high school. The only problem that he could see was that tests across classes seemed to fall around the same time every three weeks or so. Grant thought if that's the worst of it, then there's no problem.

He put his papers away in the newly organized, Container Store setup on his desk. Grant wondered how long his desk would remain this neat. He quickly glanced around the tiny room and decided to take a walk around campus so he could get a lay of the land.

It was a gorgeous day. As he walked, he thought about being away at school, how his life was now really about to start in earnest. Grant also wondered how well he would do in college. Everyone always told him he was smart because things just came easy to him in school. And he noticed how supportive his parents were. Even while checking in to school, he saw many students there on their own, without family, and wondered where their parents were. Grant was thankful that he had the support of his family, and knew that he could turn to them if anything went haywire at school.

But still, he wondered. There were new people to meet, grades to attain, laundry to do. The more Grant pondered this life transition, he realized that he didn't question his ability to be successful. He knew he could be. But then what was that nagging feeling that he had telling him that he still may not do well? Grant didn't know, but he turned to the athlete in him and blocked out that negative feeling in order to focus on the positives.

The first two weeks of school were uneventful for Grant. He was attending his classes and engaging with the classes when he could. He was happy because he seemed to find a groove for when he could do laundry when the washers were actually open and available. He also started to make friends on his floor. They would hang out at night and play spades and other card games to kill time. Some of the guys on his floor seemed to like drinking quite a bit, but Grant always turned it down.

While Grant did drink in high school, he never smoked pot. And he didn't drink that often in high school either. He was an athlete, and wanted to be sure that he could always perform as he should. So he mostly abstained from substance use. Further, he was never really a fan of how it made him feel, so that was also a deterrent for him as well. His new friends didn't get drunk or anything, just a couple of beers at 10:00 p.m. after their work was done and while they played cards. They all knew they were underage and could get in a ton of trouble for having alcohol in the dorms. But his friends' theory was that if they didn't get out of hand, they wouldn't get caught. Still, Grant thought he didn't want to engage in that. He really wanted to focus on school.

Grant did have some early morning classes and was always able to get up and arrive on time. These first two weeks, he was able to prove to himself that he was able to manage school well. He completed all of his assignments and felt as though he was settling in nicely.

He was starting to get a little nervous though. The "first wave" as he called it, was coming soon. Next week he had tests in two business classes, a math test, and an English paper to write. Grant was reassuring himself that everything would go well as long as he worked hard at it. But that nagging feeling surfaced again.

As he looked at the dates that the paper and tests were due, Grant encountered his first major struggle. He hadn't missed a class or assignment and felt like he understood the material. But he just couldn't figure out how to manage his time. At home, his parents would always be helping him organize his academic life, all the way through his senior year. They said they knew he was really smart, but they didn't want his poor organizational skills to leave him with no time to study, and then not be successful on a test. Grant never argued with them because when he followed what plans they laid out for him, he always did incredibly well. Eventually, he started working on autopilot. Between his coaches always being clear what the practice and game schedule was for sports, and his parents outlining what he needed to do for school, he just followed what was in front of him.

Now, though, Grant was realizing that he hadn't ever had to do this himself. What if he did poorly? What if his way of doing things didn't go well at all? What was he going to do?

Grant pushed these thoughts out of his head and tried to make a plan. He would scratch and scribble on a homemade calendar, but nothing he was writing was making sense to him. Every minute or so, he would crumple the sheet of paper that he was writing on and start over again.

"Deep breaths," he said aloud. The first wave was beginning in two days, and he didn't have a plan. After an hour of unrelenting focus, he put together what seemed like a plan that made sense. Grant knew it would have to do as he just couldn't waste more time planning.

Grant packed his books and walked to the library to start studying. As he found a quiet place among the stacks of books, he was amazed at the number of students there studying. He began imagining how they all must know what they're doing and are going to do much better on their first tests of the year than he will. Again, Grant had to push the negative thoughts out of his head and focus. He only had two days until this whole thing started.

He studied hard. If he wasn't in class or eating meals, he was studying. More than anything, he wanted to prove to himself that he could manage his academic work well. Test taking was the final step.

As he was studying in his dorm the night before the first of his exams, he realized that there were concepts in his math class that he just didn't understand. Grant did many problems in the book, but continued to run into the same problems. He had no idea how to solve them. Panic began to set in.

Grant noticed that his palms were getting sweaty and his heart rate definitely started picking up. Grant became swallowed up by his anxiety and told himself that he was going to fail. He wasn't feeling good about himself at all. At that moment, there was a knock on his door. Grant welcomed the interruption and rose from his chair to open the door.

"Hey, there you are! We need a fourth for spades, you in?" asked Bulge (his name was Eli, but they called him Bulge because of his size).

Grant thought a moment. He needed to decompress and thought a few games of cards wouldn't hurt.

"Sure, I'll play."

They walked down the hall and joined Russ and David.

Grant exchanged the usual pleasantries and sat down across from Bulge, who would be his partner for this round of spades.

"Anyone want a beer?" David asked.

"Sure," said Bulge and Russ.

"What the hell, I will too," Grant said.

The others looked surprised.

"What? I drink. Just haven't felt like it in a while," Grant defended himself.

"Great, let's deal," David said.

Game three had ended, and Grant was now opening his fourth beer at 10:30 p.m. He knew he had to study for his test, but just couldn't find the motivation to get up now that he had a few beers.

"I gotta finish up some work," said Russ (who had one beer).

"I guess the fun is over then," Bulge stated.

The four of them rose, and Grant not so sneakily hid his beer under his shirt as he walked back to his room. When he returned, Jon still wasn't there, presumably in the library. "How was that kid staying so focused?" he wondered.

Grant sat down at his desk again, but he couldn't focus on math. He flipped through the pages in the math textbook, and as he looked at them, he convinced himself that he really did know the material better than he initially thought. With that, he got in bed and closed his eyes.

The next morning, Grant awoke and Jon was already gone. "That guy is machine," he said to himself.

Grant opened his math book and came crashing back to earth. He realized how little he actually knew for the math test. He took a deep breath and realized that there were many sections that he did understand. But the most recent problems they had been working on in class were going to be the majority of the test, and he didn't get it. He had no idea how he was going to pass this test.

He looked at the clock. The digital face said 9:15 a.m. Class was at 10:00 a.m. Grant figured all he could do was go and try. He threw on some clothes, grabbed his books, and walked to class. He was reminding himself to think positively, that rarely were things ever as bad he thought. But the nagging thought was coming again, the one that said that he wouldn't do well.

As he sat in class, staring at the test, he knew he was screwed. Grant didn't get it. No matter how hard he tried, he didn't get it.

He did his best. When the bell rang, he stood up with everyone else in the class, and turned his test in to the professor.

Grant was overwhelmed and couldn't think clearly. He knew he had just failed that test, which was a major problem. He also had three more tests to take. There was no way that he could focus on studying for those tests knowing how this first one went. He could not control his emotions and thoughts well enough to block out this experience and refocus himself to the next challenges. This again is where his parents would just direct him.

"Why can't someone tell me what to do next," Grant said to himself, quietly but emotionally. There were still a lot people around.

Grant was feeling desperate. He had no idea what his next steps should be in light of this failure. He didn't trust what he had outlined, didn't trust that he had the ability to organize himself, and didn't trust himself to be able to retain any information that he studied. His parents and all his teachers spoke about in high school was the importance of earning good grades in college, and how that success sets a person up for a great life.

His experience now was that success may be impossible. If he can't make it through his first tests in college, how in the world will he be able to earn good grades and have a great life? Grant didn't see it. Not only was he desperate, but he was starting to feel hopeless.

Grant walked into his dorm room, which was empty again.

"How does he do it??" Grant said to himself regarding his roommate. He only saw his roommate having his act together because he seemed to be studying all of the time.

Grant glanced at his roommate's desk and noticed that there were some recent tests that Jon had taken placed there. He picked them up and saw that Jon had earned As on each. Grant put the tests back where he found them and turned to sit on his bed.

Grant put his head in hands. He didn't cry (he never cried). But if there was a time when he would, this was one of them. He felt like the only one who couldn't be successful in college. The last thing he wanted to talk about with his parents at Christmas time, when he returned home from school, was how poorly he did academically. And he really didn't want to admit that he needed their help to tell him what to do in order to turn things around for himself.

Eventually he looked up. Grant knew he had a choice. He really wanted to just quit. Just quit, fail all of these tests, and then try again in the next wave. There was one test the next day, and two the following day. Grant took a deep breath and decided to try. One test at a time.

His next test was an Intro to Business class. Grant felt like he had a good handle on that test. When he was studying, he felt positive that his initial feelings were being reinforced, and it was coming easy to him. Because this experience was going well, he decided not study for his other tests yet. He wanted to feel confident, and opening another textbook scared him into thinking that it could all disappear... quickly.

Grant strode into class the next morning feeling incredibly confident. When he received the test he quickly glanced through all of the questions. No surprises. This was positive. He was one of the first ones done, turned his test in, and left class early. He was feeling great.

"Maybe I'm overreacting. Maybe I can do this on my own." Grant was starting to believe it.

Grant was now striding through campus with an air of confidence. The more he thought about it, the better he was feeling. As he walked to his English class, he was at a place where he thought he belonged.

"Class, before we start," said his professor, "please turn your papers in to me now so I don't have to collect them at the end."

Grant felt like he'd been hit by a train.

The paper. The freaking paper! His professor said it and it all came flying back to him. He had four tests *and a paper.* When he put together his plan he only wrote down the four tests!

Grant didn't know what to do. He just sat there, watching all of the other students turn in their papers. The feelings of desperation and hopelessness came storming back. He couldn't pay attention throughout class. When it was over, Grant still hadn't yet decided if he should tell the professor what his situation was, or just leave and deal with it some other time. He decided on the latter and started walking back to his dorm.

Empty dorm room again! Where was Jon? Not that he would talk much to him. But how could someone be this busy?

Grant sat at his desk and tried to study for the two tests he had the next day, but couldn't focus. After trying for about an hour, he quit. He was convinced that whatever grade he received if he studied, would be the same grade he would get if he didn't study.

That night his buddies on the floor were going out for hamburgers and he decided to go. They were able to be served beer as well because the server didn't bother asking for identification. Since he didn't care about the tests the next day, Grant decided he would drink more liberally than he typically would.

His friends helped him back to his room that night and he passed out on his bed. When he awoke the next morning with a vicious headache, his roommate was gone again. He sat up slowly, found some water, and began heartily drinking what was left. He took a deep breath, rose, and knew he had to deal with these tests.

They went as expected. Bad.

Grant felt incredibly hopeless and didn't know what to do. He was questioning how he didn't learn how to stay organized in high school. How did his parents let him go away without him knowing some of these basic things? And now what? Who should he talk do about his current performance? He had to talk to someone. Grant didn't know what to say either way. His parents had always managed the discussions with the teachers, coaches, or others who were in charge for him. He always appreciated them handling these things. It could be intimidating for him and it was nice for him not to have to worry about it.

As he opened the door to his room, he saw Jon sitting at his desk.

"You're alive!" Grant said sarcastically.

"Sure am," Jon smiled in return.

"Where do you go every day? You're, like, never here," Grant put his question out there.

"Do you remember at orientation they gave us that huge packet of resources that the college has?" Jon started to explain.

"Yeah. That just has the health clinic and things like that," Grant thought he knew what Jon was talking about.

"It does, but it also had all these opportunities to receive tutoring and help if students ever have a hard time in their classes."

Was Jon saying that he got a lot of extra help? Grant couldn't believe it.

"I always had a hard time in high school with understanding concepts. But once I got it, I did well. I just needed extra help actually getting it. Know what I mean?" John continued.

Grant nodded.

"Early in high school, my parents helped me get set up with teachers and tutors. But once the middle of 10th grade came around, they told me I had to start managing it myself. So I started meeting with teachers on my own, asking questions, getting help, just being sure that I understood what was happening in class. This helped me keep my grades up. When I got here, I figured I should try to keep doing the same things that got me here, so I did. The people are really nice and incredibly helpful. My thought is that after this semester I may not need to go as often as I do now. But I didn't want to take any chances at the start of the year."

"Wow," was all Grant could muster for a moment. "So it's that helpful?"

"Absolutely. How are things going for you?" Jon asked.

Grant took a deep breath and let Jon know all that he had been through the past few weeks.

"I'm sorry to hear that, Grant. I really am. Did anyone ever help you learn how to handle this stuff in high school?"

Grant shook his head. "My parents mostly took care of it all for me. I just did what everyone told me to do. Once I got here and had to figure it out on my own, it got hard. Laundry is one thing, but these classes are hard."

"I'm going to head over to the tutoring center soon. Want to come with me? Maybe we can grab some food after?"

"That would be great. Thanks."

Grant was finally feeling hopeful that someone could help guide him out of the mess that he had created.

The Lesson

The story is the positive version of what happens to so many kids when they go away to school. Typically, students go away to college without having to take ownership of their lives until the day that college begins. When they do, they find that they are wildly unprepared and don't know why. Most, if not all, are intelligent people who have experienced significant successes in their lives to that point. And that's what confuses them. They see their past outcomes and can't understand why they are not achieving the same outcomes in college. The answer lies not in how smart or capable they are, but in applying what, if anything, have they been taught.

We see this play out with Grant and Jon. Grant clearly is struggling with managing his academic life. He had good outcomes in the past, but with significant assistance from his parents. They never handed him the reins to his own life until his first day of college. Contrast that with Jon, who was aware of the help he needed because his parents passed the reins to him in 10th grade. We see that even though their struggles are similar, they are managing them very differently.

Grant is assuming that he should be able to manage his struggles effectively. His assumption is coming from the place that he's always had successful outcomes, so he should be able to achieve them now.

Jon made the assumption that he couldn't manage his struggles well on his own. More than that, he assumed that he would have struggles *because he always had*. Jon could have just as easily told himself that he'd been getting so much help over the years that he would try it himself once he arrived at college, but he didn't. He was able to accept his reality of how he learns, and continued to embrace the struggle in college. This allowed him to continue to practice the same strategies that he used throughout high school in order to be successful.

First Year Fails

This story is a very important one. Over the years, my practice has worked with countless young adults who went away to college only to fail out after their first year. The steps down this road most often begin because they can't balance the workload and freedom that college life offers. Once a negative, academic experience occurs, students then struggle to accept their new reality that things are not going well for them, and start to avoid the problems. They'll stop attending classes, stop doing work, and then eventually increase their use of drugs (most often marijuana) and alcohol. At that point, there is nothing that will change.

These students then hide the reality from their parents and friends so they can keep the facade of success in full force. But as with all facades, they eventually come crashing down. For these students, this happens at the end of the semester when a parent asks to actually see the report card, rather than just get a self-report from the student about how they are doing (since the student has been lying to the parent for some time).

Once the realities become clear, students may struggle with a substance abuse issue in addition to depression or anxiety related issues on top of the already complicated academic situation they put themselves in. This can potentially be a disastrous scenario for these students because they now have to start over. They live at home, attend a community college, and obtain jobs. Students with fragile egos oftentimes can't cope with this reality, and the substance abuse issues worsen. Those who are able to accept their reality, and understand full well how their choices contributed to their reality, can learn from this experience so they can have a life that is not impeded by what has occurred.

We can see from the story that a common factor in how Grant and Jon experienced college was their parents.

Grant's parents never did let him figure out how to cope with his own struggles independently. They owned his struggle throughout high school by organizing him and communicating with school personnel as necessary.

Jon's parents did the opposite. They allowed him to take ownership and control of his life, which Jon was able to do so successfully.

As kids get older, parents have to start acting less like parents, and more like coaches, to their children. Grant's parents stayed parents. They took care of his difficulties and assisted him as much as they could while Grant learned nothing from their actions. Because of this, Grant didn't have a foundation for how to manage his situations when circumstances arose that he needed to address on his own.

Coaching Versus Covering

Most important to recognize is that Grant's parents were focused only on outcomes. They just wanted to make sure that Grant was set up to have good grades. But they missed the point. They missed that while

Grant was achieving the grades, he had no idea how to sustain his progress if the supports disappeared. Grant didn't even realize how important learning the process was because he was so focused on the outcomes as well.

This is why focusing on process and experience is so important at a young age. When parents only focus on outcomes throughout a child's life, they are taking away virtually every potential learning experience from the child. The child feels great, but has no idea why because the parents are propping him up to ensure that he stays that way. But eventually the parents disappear, like when the now grown child goes to college, and the child doesn't know what to do.

The solution is what Jon's parents did. They knew he had struggles. But they also knew that they couldn't be there forever. So they let Jon get involved in the process well *before* he left for college. Many parents feel that it's a risk, but the costs and benefits must be weighed out. If a child is engaging in the process at a young age, and working through their mistakes, there will certainly be times when the child messes up. The mistake could even be large.

But as a parent, would you rather have the opportunity to coach your child through mistakes when he is young and in school? Or make your child figure them out by himself when they are older and you are not available to them for help?

This is what happened with Jon and Grant. Jon was coached through high school. Grant was not. Jon knew what he needed in order to be successful when he went to college. Grant did not.

This is the setup that many parents do to their kids. They prop them up, tell them they're great, tell them not to worry, take care of all the issues, and then they fall flat on their faces six weeks into college because they have no idea how to take care of themselves.

And the sad part is that it's so preventable. But parents continue to believe that somehow the only thing that proves their worth as a parent is how easy their child's life is. Therefore, they spend their time protecting their children, not teaching them. They spend their time making excuses for them or justifying their behaviors to others.

But for the parents who consistently hold their children accountable and demand them to achieve the expectations that the parents have put forth, they are successful parents. They will push their children to not only be successful in the various areas of their life; they will also *teach* their children how to be successful independently.

And that is what virtually all parents want of their children: To be successful, adaptive, and independent in their personal and professional lives. But in order for this to happen, parents have to be purposeful in how they steer their children. Success doesn't happen by accident. Parents can't cover up their children's mistakes, and then be surprised that their children can't function on their own.

Parents often cover up for their children until they graduate high school. After that, the child is exposed to the world. Whatever skills they have or lack to that point will be clear as day. It's our job to prepare them for that day, not protect them until that day.

Chapter 9

The Culmination

The Story

Bill was staring at his email inbox with the dozens of messages that required a response from him, but he couldn't focus enough to reply. He had interviewed with the Head of Human Resources, Greg, and the Chief Operating Officer, Nancy, for the open position of Director of Risk Management. It was a great opportunity, one that would come with an increase in responsibility and, if not more important, compensation.

Today, Bill was to hear about whether he would get the position. He had been considered for other promotions in the past, but hadn't been able to close the deal. The feedback he had received in the past was that he was too focused on his department, and didn't consider the needs of the organization often enough.

Bill thought that was just a B.S. reason for them to give the roles to other people. He *knew* he was a great boss. He did everything he could to make sure that his staff liked him. So what if there were times that it cost the company money or made things challenging for another department? It was hard to manage 20 people, and he had to do it his own way.

But he also knew that his superiors were frustrated by his lack of investment in a huge, company-wide project to improve efficiencies across the departments. They wanted him to spend a ton of hours on reviewing all of these procedures. But he believed those hours would be better spent engaging with his staff. They needed him more than his superiors did. And if his superiors were unhappy with his decision, then so be it.

That was a little harsh. Bill knew that he wasn't great at procedural things. He was much better at relating to his staff. He was worried that being involved in that massive procedure evaluation and overhaul would've exposed virtually all of his weaknesses as a manager. If he showed his superiors where his weaknesses really were, how could he ever be promoted? Bill believed the most advantageous move for himself was to stick to his areas of strength, and avoid the projects and interactions as much as possible that would show where his weaknesses were.

His superiors had tried to speak with him about his weaknesses, and he knew it. This was frustrating for him as he never could understand why they always wanted to spend so much time with him talking about his negatives. It's like they never saw all of the positive things that he has achieved. Bill knew he wasn't perfect, but he thought it was fair to expect validation for his work and not just a focus on the things he had to improve on. He looked over at the "Employee of the Year" he had previously been awarded. A lot had changed since then, Bill thought.

He had been in his new role as a Manager for a year at that time. He had received this level of prestigious recognition because, as the company was expanding, the effort he put into his staff and department was exemplary. Bill felt great about the recognition. He read what was engraved on the plague "Thank you for all of your hard work this year. We look forward to many years of growth together."

Bill thought about that. He always took "growth" literally, meaning that the company would literally grow with people and equipment. He didn't consider that growth also may have meant intellectual, intuitive, or other intangible growth as leader. He brushed the thought away.

"Those things don't matter," he said aloud to himself.

Bill was convinced that all that did matter was his ability to advocate for his department and generate money for his company. That's all that mattered to him, and he did both well.

Little did Bill know that while he sat at his desk, convincing himself that he was right candidate for the role, a very real discussion about this topic was occurring at the same time, in the same building, two floors above his office.

"What do you think we should do? We have to make a decision," Greg, the head of Human Resources said to Nancy, the Chief

Operations Officer. They were meeting because they recently completed interviews of current employees to fill a Director level position which would be in charge of overseeing multiple departments within their company, Vand Industries.

"Let's look at our top three people," Nancy began. "We have Rick, who has led his department for two years now and has been outstanding in training his staff and remaining profitable. But he has struggled with communicating with other departments when necessary. We have Bill, who has managed his department for five years. He always does everything he's asked, and does a great job with every task he's given. But he struggles to see how influential his department is within the company. He doesn't understand that we need him to look at the big picture sometimes, not just through the lens of his department. Then we have Mary. She's run her department for three years, and has been outstanding. She leads her people, understands the right time to go outside of her department to complete tasks, but also knows when to stay in the box. Pretty impressive, actually. Staff from other departments like and respect her."

"If I'm reading you right, it sounds like we think Mary is the best fit?"

Nancy paused to think. "Yes, I believe she is. Her ability to understand the nuances of when to invest in her department versus when to push outside of her department are just head and shoulders above the other two candidates. I think she is exactly the type of thinker we need at the director level right now."

"But you paused first. Why?"

Nancy nodded. "I did, but not because I was unsure about Mary. You may not be aware, Greg, because it was before your time, but this will be the third time Bill will be passed over for a promotion. While he's not the best fit for the director level, he's a great manager. I'm concerned that we may lose him if he's passed over again."

"Makes sense to worry about that. But has anyone spoken with him before about why he didn't get the other promotions?"

"Yes, many times. It's the same reason as now. While he's shown improvement, he just hasn't been able to get to where we need him to be. He's become a great manager, but I don't know that I'd want him involved in larger decisions. The biggest issue with him is that he's so focused on his department, and what's 'right and fair' to them, while struggling to see how his department fits within the whole company.

"Do you remember when we did that investment in equipment about a year ago?" Greg nodded. "Bill was in an uproar for about two weeks because his department was receiving only 10 percent of the budgeted dollars. His argument was that there were four main departments, so his should receive 25 percent. He struggled to see that the needs of the other departments outweighed the needs of his own financially. And even though he struggled with seeing that, what made it harder was that the investment in the other departments would actually end up lightening the workload in his department."

"I remember that. We estimated we would be able to cut overtime by almost 50 percent in Bill's department by those investments. Not only would that save the company money, but it would allow for his staff to leave on time more often so they could have a better quality of life," Greg recalled.

"Right, but Bill just couldn't see it. He kept staying focused on how I 'didn't want him to succeed' or some garbage like that. It's just so confusing. On the one hand he's a great manager. It seems he should be able to make the leap to Director, but his focus on himself just gets in the way."

"It's funny you say that. It seems like the times when we've met for our Leadership Development sessions, he presents in many of the same ways that you're describing. I just thought it was because I was the HR guy. But he really did not like acknowledging any weakness that he had, and seemed frustrated that we weren't spending more time discussing the positive things he'd accomplished. I know I communicated to him how well he was doing in some areas, but the purpose of the meetings was to challenge him so he could grow, not validate his comfort zone," Greg seemed to understand Nancy's perspective.

"Let's get Mary in and tell her the good news. Then, let's get Bill and Rick here soon after to explain our decision," Nancy was ready to move forward.

The day went by at a snail's pace. Bill hadn't heard anything about a decision, but then his phone rang.

"Hello this Bill," he tried to sound like he was playing it cool.

"Hey Bill? It's Greg from HR. Are you available to come up to my office?"

"Sure, be there in a minute."

"Great".

Click

Bill had many thoughts running through his head. Did Greg sound excited? Was he just going through the motions? These questions were floating in his head as he ran up the staircases, rather than waiting for the elevator. When he arrived at Greg's office, he saw the door was open. Nancy motioned for him to come in. As he did, he closed the door behind him and sat down at the small table in the office. Everyone was quiet so Greg could finish the call he was on.

"Okay," Greg said as he hung up the phone. "Bill, I'm sure you know that we asked you here to let you know the outcome of the interviews that you participated in for the Director position."

Bill nodded eagerly, but not too eagerly.

"You've done a wonderful job with us in your manager role," Greg continued. "But, unfortunately, we're not able to move you into the Director role at this time."

"Why?" was all Bill could muster as a question.

"Well," Nancy began. "I know you've put in for a promotion a couple of times previously. I believe we've tried to help you grow the skills necessary to be a Director. It just seems that your intense focus on the areas that are important to you get in the way of being able to look at the needs of the company. Being a Director means being able to step outside of oneself and look at everything that happens at once, not just on what is important to you. And this has come out not only through the leadership sessions that Greg has had with you. I know I was disappointed at your investment in the procedure review we conducted a few months ago. I don't know if you meant to, but the message you sent was that you didn't want to be involved in the project, even though we needed you to be."

"I don't understand," Bill was dumbfounded. "I work so hard to support my staff, to ensure that the department functions so well. It seems like you don't want to see me succeed."

There was silence in the room as Greg and Nancy looked at each other, playing a game of visual chicken to see who would have to address Bill's comment. Nancy spoke first.

"Bill, we really don't want to debate any of this. But it's times like now which is why you didn't get the role. I mean, we've talked so often about thinking for the good of the company, not your people. You've made some questionable decisions over the years, but you were always coming from the right place."

"What do you mean? Like what?" Bill challenged.

"Well, most recently, you changed that one piece of the process on how to deliver our items to our customers on your own in order to simplify the work for your team," Nancy explained.

"And I did! It cut down our work by about 15 percent. I would think I would be praised for that."

"However," Nancy continued, "it just came to our attention that you've created twice the work for two other departments."

She sighed.

"I just don't know how else to say it. When you act independently, it's in the interests of you or your staff, and you don't consult with others. When we want your input on the process things, it's like you remove yourself completely and don't get involved. If we tell you you've done a great job at something, you act like that's not good enough recognition. If we coach you through areas where you struggle, you act like you don't want to hear it. And if there's not some type of 'instant success' after an initiative you take, it seems like you become frustrated easily and don't take on the challenge. But then it seems like you may actually try when I have to literally tell you to be a part of a task. I'm not trying to be hard on you; I'm just trying to be honest. You're a great manager and we want you to be able to continue to grow here," Nancy thought Bill deserved the truth, so she put it all out there. After all, this was the third time he'd been passed over for a promotion. He needed to hear the hard truth.

"I don't know what to say," Bill said. He felt attacked, unappreciated, and more certain than ever that Nancy didn't want him in a high level role within the company.

"Please think about what she said," Greg chimed in. "If you can understand what she's saying, we can certainly work together so you can be better positioned when the next opportunity presents itself."

Bill thanked them for their time and effort, shook their hands, and left the office.

"I don't think he gets it. I tried to be as honest as I could. He could be great, he really could. But he's so caught up in these other things that don't matter, I don't know if he'll ever be able to challenge himself and continue to grow," Nancy concluded.

"Well, it happened again!" Bill blurted out as he walked into the kitchen. He had just returned home from work. His wife, Kim, was helping their oldest child, Anna, with her homework while their youngest, Tia, was watching TV.

"What?" Kim asked a look of concern on her face.

"I got passed over for another promotion. I've been with that company for five years and they just won't allow me to move up. At this point, I feel like Nancy or Greg, or both of them, are working against me."

"I thought you said you all got along well? It doesn't seem like they are trying to hold you back. You've had other opportunities to interview for other positions there. Did they tell you why you were passed over?"

"Just something about how while I do good work, they believe that I just don't invest in the whole company and tend to remain focused on my department. But what do they expect me to do? I'm hired to be a manager of a large department, and I manage that department really well. How can I take care of my department and invest in the whole company at the same time? That's why I think they don't want me to move up."

"That makes sense. Have you tried to learn more about what they are referring to?" Kim asked.

"I have! They just don't understand what I need from them in order to do my job well!"

"But, Bill, what have you learned from them?"

This question stumped him. Kim was always great about challenging him, but this one was hard. Maybe that was the point. He hadn't learned anything.

"You know, we've talked about it. You have a way of always wanting to do your own thing around here without letting me know what your plan is. Like when you up and decided to buy a new car that was more expensive, but didn't talk to me first," Kim added.

"And the times when we have a difficult thing to figure out with the kids. You act like you're engaged, but in the end I'm the one who has to figure it all out. We've talked about these things quite a few times. But it seems like it's really hard for you to make the changes once we talk about it. Neither of us is perfect and I love you for who you are. But you have to start wondering whether some of these things are getting in the way of you being successful at work. You know there are times when I get frustrated with you about these same things here at home."

"But that's home and it's supposed to be hard. You know that I care about you and the kids. But I'm just being myself. Is who I am really that bad?" Bill came home looking for support, but Kim getting on his case now, too, wasn't helping.

"That's not what anyone is saying!" Kim was getting frustrated. "You don't have to play the martyr all the time. Just take a breath and hear what I'm saying. You're great at many things, Bill. But you have to work on remaining engaged with things at home, even when you're not interested in the situation or topic. Let's face it; if it's not about you, you struggle to stay fully engaged."

Bill sat with that comment from his wife and thought about it. Maybe that's what Nancy and Greg were trying to stay to him earlier. That he only gets invested in the things that he likes. And he only stays invested when he can virtually be assured of success. That's why he backs away from engaging at home. Everything is always changing, and there's no way to no know how right or wrong a decision may be. So he backs off and lets Kim make the final call on everything.

He hated hearing constructive criticism about himself because he hated how that made him feel. He always much preferred hearing the positive and couldn't understand how other people could be so comfortable with challenging their shortcomings. With that, and the other things Kim, Greg, and Nancy had said to him, he realized that he had a lot of work to do if he was ever going to move up in his current company. He also knew he had a ton to do in order to build trust with his wife to assure her that he wouldn't run from life's problems when they arose, would remain engaged, and would be a team player with her in finding the solution.

The Lesson

This story is not uncommon. We have a person, Bill, who is working hard and appears to be successful in his life professionally and personally. But we also see that there are major skills gaps that he can't intuitively cover. If we look at Bill's professional experience, he's been passed over multiple times for a promotion mainly because he was unable to evolve. His bosses clearly outlined to him what they wanted from him in his current role so they could justify moving him to a higher level, and he continually was unable to show these skills. His bosses were invested in his growth, but he was not able to use their feedback in ways that were constructive or helpful to him or the company.

On a personal level, these issues were present there as well, but to a less consequential level. Bill's wife, Kim, was clearly annoyed by some of the behaviors that Bill would intermittently display, but not to such a large extent that she would characterize her family life as being unhappy. But Bill talking about his work experiences opened the door for her to draw comparisons to their personal life well. So why is it that someone who, on the surface, can look so successful, but directly underneath have the struggles that he does in his personal and professional lives?

Let's look at the points that were brought up in the story and compare them to the points of previous chapters. How kids are raised and what they are taught directly influences their perceptions and behaviors into adulthood.

Problems with Continuous Positive Reinforcement

Nancy laid out to Bill in an exasperated fashion why he didn't receive his promotion. Let's break down her comments. First, she said, "When you act independently, it's in the interests of you or your staff, and you don't consult with others."

This speaks to the self-centered nature that children develop when they are always highlighted with the positive. Children who experience life as though they never do anything wrong, continue to believe that will hold true into adulthood. Their behaviors tend to be self-centered, or interest-centered, because they continue to crave the constant feeling of positive reinforcement or validation.

Bill, while most likely not realizing it, was craving the praise he would receive from his staff when he acted in ways that made them feel important. This validation then motivated him again to continue to make similar decisions. Because of this, it became harder for him to step outside of his own experiences and make decisions for the good of the company, which is what his bosses needed most from him. And the vicious cycle continued. Even though his bosses were investing in him to develop and enhance his leadership skills, Bill was never able to own that he needed to have this emotional experience at work. Therefore, all of the investment that his bosses gave him would be wasted.

And Bill's lack of consultation with other people on his decisions further cements his position that he needs the positive reinforcement for his own personal gain. While one may say that not consulting others for advice on decisions may be ignorant, I would argue that there was a significant part of Bill that was scared to talk to anyone at work about work related decisions. There was a part of him that knew they would tell him to do something else, breaking his cycle of positive reinforcement.

While Bill may have been making decisions motivated by his own desire for positive validation, he most likely was aware of the pattern and didn't want to give it up. In my clinical experience, people tend to be more insightful than their behaviors would suggest. I think Bill would know that if he talked about his decisions with others, he would be forced to take other courses of action that wouldn't feel as good.

There are a number of people who crave positive reinforcement so much that they can't form functional relationships with other adults. There are people who can't handle negative emotions so they turn to anything to stay positive, including drugs, multiple sexual relationships, and other things that will externally reinforce to them that their lives are okay.

Anxiety and Avoidance

Second, Nancy said, "When we want your input on the process things, it's like you remove yourself completely and don't get involved."

This builds off the first scenario where Bill is constantly looking for positive reinforcement and knows that being involved on a group project may challenge that. But it goes a step further and goes to a place where Bill's anxiety is directly called out by Nancy. She recognizes that Bill wants to run and hide from a situation that is going to create much anxiety in him. The frustrating part for Nancy, the boss in this scenario, is that she wants his involvement in this process. His avoidance actually hinders the process.

But the problem here is that Bill believes his avoidance actually helps the situation, which again creates another vicious cycle. Bill avoids because he believes that it's helpful, despite feedback he's receiving to the contrary. Again, this is because Bill is *listening to his anxiety*, not the people whose feedback he values. The more Bill listens to his anxiety and gives it power, the more it creates disadvantages to him in the workplace. Listening to anxiety and giving it the authority that Bill did can be devastating.

Craving Constant Praise

Third, Nancy said, "If we tell you you've done a great job at something, you act like it's not good enough recognition."

Again, the need for constant praise. But this is where the need for praise becomes complex. When someone is in an entry level position at work, they typically receive a fair amount of praise by any one of a number of their superiors. But, as that person moves up the organizational ladder, the amount of praise that he will receive decreases because the performance expectations in his job function have increased. This then means that person is simply not being praised as much as he would like to be.

So when Bill receives praise, he's trying to get as much as he can because he feels innately like he hasn't been praised enough for other areas in his role as well. This then creates frustration for bosses because they feel like they are giving the positive reinforcement. However, the problem is that it's not even close to the degree that Bill needs it.

Which now leads to the crux of the issue. The idea is that, as children, the positive reinforcement that we receive from adults, parents, teachers, etc. eventually becomes internalized into our sense of self. But with people like Bill, who come to depend on the positive reinforcement as way to validate themselves and remain as secure as possible, they were never able to internalize that reinforcement to use when they weren't receiving the praise they would like. What this created for Bill was the constant desire for praise. It's why he needed to have good relationships from his staff. That praise was just "good enough."

But the praise he really wanted was from the people at Nancy's level of the organization, and he just wasn't going to receive it with the frequency or intensity that he would like. Therefore, his insecurity would flare up periodically. Bill was like a car driving across the country. He would need to refuel almost constantly in order to make the trip, as compared to other cars that would only refuel a handful of times. His emotional gas tank was small and he would burn fuel as quickly as it was placed in there. That insecurity drove his behaviors, which therefore caused great struggles for him in the professional world.

Bill would look at his bosses and wonder why he wasn't getting praised more often and perhaps more publicly for his work. His bosses would look at Bill and wonder why he wasn't more secure in his own choices and actions so he didn't have to depend on them as much to tell them how great he was. His bosses didn't see insecurity as a positive trait in a leader. Bill couldn't see that he was insecure.

Constructive Criticism and the Unwilling Student

Fourth, Nancy said, "If we coach you through areas where you struggle, you act like you don't want to hear it."

This goes back to the point of the second chapter which discussed feeling comfortable with guilt and shame. Receiving constructive criticism is difficult; I don't care how comfortable someone says they are with the process. It's just hard to hear someone else's experience of you or your actions as being negative, especially when the motives behind the actions may have been very positive.

It's even harder when the criticism is more of a character flaw, not just an error in judgment or thought. So to hear these things, one must be very prepared to deal with the emotions that are going to come up when negative feedback is given. Many people feel ashamed when criticism is leveled at them, and therefore spend more time trying to make themselves feel better, rather than use the feedback that they had just received constructively.

And this situation is exactly why it's so important to have the skills of managing guilt and shame. Here we have Nancy expressing to Bill her frustration with feeling like her efforts to assist him learn and get better in his role were falling on deaf ears. She was stating that she wanted him to improve, but Bill was unable to receive the help. And he ultimately put the blame on his boss with his comment of, "It seems like you don't want me to succeed."

This becomes the inherent conflict when leadership is trying to develop future leaders. The future leaders need to be able to put their egos aside and learn how to become better, regardless of how uncomfortable they may feel. Bill's inability to hear the criticism created a situation where his bosses were trying to teach an unwilling student. Eventually they metaphorically threw their hands up in frustration because they didn't know what else to do. And Bill was frustrated with them for doing so, but at the same time lacked the insight into his role through that process.

Unrealistic Expectations for Instant Success

Fifth, Nancy said, "And if there's not some type of 'instant success' after an initiative you take, it seems like you become frustrated easily and don't take on the challenge."

This speaks to the combination of Bill needing positive reinforcement and coping with anxiety. The comment here refers to a need that many people have that they'll try something only if they know they'll be successful prior to trying it. Children oftentimes think in these terms. They'll say that they won't play a sport or try art because, "If I'm not good at it, what's the point?"

Bill clearly took on the same type of thought process. He wanted to ensure quick and easy success so he could feed his need for positive reinforcement, and would avoid a task in order to settle his anxiety. Further, because of our culture of instant gratification, Bill became accustomed to thinking that "instant success" was an option more often than is realistic. so he set himself up for failure in believing that there was really a way to try something new and be good at it quickly.

Lacking Initiative

Lastly, Nancy said, "But then it seems like you may actually try when I have to literally tell you to be a part of a task."

Here, Nancy is talking about her experience that when she is explicitly directive to Bill and what she needs him to do, she gets better engagement from him. This speaks to Bill being comfortable having someone tell him what to do in order to ensure that he completes the right task and does it correctly. Nancy is saying that Bill has an inability to take initiative on a task because, like she said in the previous comment, if he's not assured success, he won't try at all. But when he is virtually "ordered" to complete a task, he will engage a little more in it.

Again, this is not a leadership trait that any company wants. Organizations desire people who want to take initiative. Leaders who have to "order" projects to be completed will get tired because of all of the thinking they are required to do. They depend on the initiative of their people to get a great amount of work complete and to recognize potential problems. Those who do better when told what to do quickly become an unwanted disturbance in the machinery of an organization, and therefore become viewed as unnecessary.

People who just want to be successful avoid taking all initiative. They find comfort in being controlled by their bosses and avoiding anxiety provoking situations. But the irony is that organizations prefer employees who are independent, assertive, adaptive, and take initiative. This is why the dependent employee struggles in an organization. Their needs are completely counterintuitive to the organization's needs, creating much conflict in the workplace because the employees and their leaders are frequently at odds.

When Parents Need Parenting

All of these traits and skills are ones that children learn as they're being raised. How well kids learn these skills are not measured through test scores, sports teams played on, recitals performed in, or a GPA. Rather, they should be evaluated when the tests don't go well, when a child fails in their area of interest, or receives a disappointing GPA. What is the child's response? What is the parents' response? We don't want our children being their own worst enemy into adulthood. Bill's situation is a relatively positive one. He held a good job and had a loving family. But he could excel so much further if he didn't get in his own way.

Bill's wife, Kim, also spoke about these things, but to a lesser level at home. She noted his impulse to "buy a car without consulting her," or disconnecting when there are challenging decisions to be made about the kids. Bill was able to allow his traits have less of an effect at home because he presumably was married to a secure spouse who was able to take on the emotional burden for him. Bill just wasn't able receive the emotional cover in the workplace. Therefore, his vulnerabilities were exposed to a much larger and meaningful extent than at home.

At home, the points that Nancy made from work still apply. Parents need to be able to teach their children these skills. But what happens when one or both parents don't possess the skills themselves? The parents then parent not to their kids' needs, but their own. What I mean is, parents will make decisions and take action based upon what helps them feel most comfortable, and not what is in the best interest of their kids.

It's pretty simple, really. If parents hate feeling anxious, they will make decisions that are anxiety avoidant for their children, creating children who aren't comfortable with anxiety. If parents aren't capable of taking responsibility for their actions, they'll raise kids who are incapable of being responsible for their actions. The list goes on. This is why it is absolutely incumbent on parents to understand what their own areas of strengths and weakness are so they can best teach their kids how to be the best adults they can be.

Chapter 10

Adaptive and Independent

The Story

"Oh crap," Rachel said aloud.

Rachel was six weeks into her new role as an Assistant Design Editor for a major magazine, and was sitting at her desk, after 5:00 p.m. on a Tuesday, working. Her desk was spotlessly clean when she started, but the papers that had piled up in such a short period of time allowed her to see how those people ended up on the TV reality show "Hoarders."

She had been working for magazine companies for six years now, since she graduated college, and loved it. What she enjoyed most was the constant challenges that it always presented. She didn't know why it was, but she loved solving problems as they related to magazines, publishing, and the intricate details that went along with it. She was hoping to be leave by 7:00 p.m. But this email that she just received said otherwise.

The email was from her boss, Michael. She liked him well enough so far, but wasn't yet able to make a final judgement. People in the magazine world could be cutthroat.

He had sent the following note to her and the two other Assistant's at the magazine:

We had to move up the deadline for next month's issue a week from next Thursday to this Thursday, two days from now. Something with the printing company. Adjust your schedule accordingly.

Michael

While this was certainly a major change in plan, it could have been worse. Rachel's experience in this world was that timelines could always change at a moment's notice. It was always amazing to her how many people she had worked with over the past few years who weren't able to adjust to constant motion that occurred in their role. This change in timeline certainly posed some new challenges for her. Not only was she in for a few late nights, but she'd have to speak with her husband, Dan, about how her schedule would be changing, so they could plan appropriate coverage for their 14-month old daughter, Chloe.

She picked up the phone to call her husband.

"Hello?" Dan didn't enter Rachel's new work phone number into his phone yet.

"Hey, it's me. How're things at home?"

"Good. I just picked up Chloe and was going to feed her. What's up?"

"Well, I just had a major deadline get moved from next Thursday to this Thursday. I'm screwed for the next few nights. Okay, if I come home late?" Rachel knew it would be, but she had to ask.

"Of course. We're in good shape here. Get done what you need to. Does this free you up then for this weekend now that the deadline moved?" Dan asked.

"It should. I don't anticipate any changes in my schedule. This is about as big as it should get."

"Great, we'll take Chloe down to that new park or something," Dan liked to think ahead.

"Sounds fun! Don't wait up, I'll be late."

"Got it, good luck. Bye."

"Bye."

Rachel loved how Dan could adjust to massive changes in his schedule or responsibilities with no fanfare. Rachel would speak to her friends and listen to their frustrations about how much of a struggle it was for them to either communicate changes in plans to their spouses, or how much they didn't like it when people changed plans on them. Rachel always thought of that as ironic, but never shared her point of view as she didn't believe her friends would find the situation as entertaining as she did.

She wouldn't be surprised if Dan told her later that he had surprised her by picking up some great sushi from the new place that opened up down the street from their apartment for dinner tonight. Dan understood that even though he may try to do nice things for Rachel, her schedule wouldn't always cooperate. He never gave her a hard time about it, and that just helped her appreciate their family more and not get bogged down by the problems that her work life created.

Rachel was just starting to get to work on the following month's issue when there was a knock on her door. She was startled as she wasn't expecting anyone, and certainly didn't know anyone all that well as of yet.

"Come in!" Rachel said almost too enthusiastically.

"Hi, sorry to bother you. I'm Debbie, one of the other Assistant Editors here."

"Right! We met at the meeting last week. I think you were on vacation when I started and our paths haven't really crossed. Good to see you again!"

"Same here. Look, did you get that email from Michael?"

"I did. What a pain. But, that's life in this world, right?"

Debbie looked surprised.

"Well, you're taking this with a good attitude because it's the first time it's happened to you here. This B.S. happens ALL THE TIME. Michael is incredibly unorganized and he doesn't respect our time at all," Debbie said defiantly.

"Wow. I wasn't aware that these deadline changes were an issue," Rachel was concerned.

"Well, they are. Anyway, I was thinking about having all of the Assistant Editors meet with Michael's boss, Erin, about this issue. Are you in?"

Rachel was put on the spot.

"I'm not totally sure. Can I think about it?"

"Sure, but not for too long. If we're going to meet with her, we should do it Thursday, after we meet the deadline for the new issue."

"Okay, I'll let you know by then."

Debbie nodded and walked out. Rachel took a deep breath.

There was always someone like that in the workplace, right? She thought to herself. Debbie was only one person. Who knows what the history was between her and Michael? It was always disconcerting to hear people talk like Debbie did. It just made her question her decision to work here, even though this magazine had the best reputation around.

Rachel took another deep breath.

She decided that she would finish what she could for the new issue tonight, and head home a little early so she could talk to Dan about what happened. She didn't want to get in the middle of a political office war after only six weeks in her new role.

She got home a little after 10:00 p.m., and Dan was watching *Cheers* reruns on Netflix.

"I wish we were alive when this show was on. Norm and Cliff are hilarious."

"You know I can't get into that show. It's too stupid for me."

"I know, you're above this comedy," Dan said sarcastically. "You're home earlier that I thought. Got more done than you thought?"

"I wish. A big thing came up and I'm not totally sure what to do about it."

Dan paused his show, which left Sam and Woody in the middle of an animated discussion.

"What's up?" he asked.

Rachel told him the story of the deadline change and Debbie's subsequent visit to her office.

"I don't want to get caught up in this whole thing. But I get the feeling that I'm not going to have a choice. I need to think about the best way to go about handling this, and I need to do something tomorrow because Thursday I'm going to have to know my stance so I can tell Debbie. I already don't like her," Rachel vented.

"Well, what does your gut tell you?"

"I think Debbie is playing her own angle. I get that the deadline being moved is frustrating, but I don't know why she would want to go at this so aggressively, especially with someone as new to the company as I am. If I had been there a long time and shared in her experience, I could understand. But not so much in this case." Rachel was surprised by how firm she felt this.

"Do you think it would be okay for you to talk to Michael about this? I mean, obviously not tell him what Debbie had said, but rather just in the name of 'asking questions as the new person'?" Dan liked brainstorming.

"I think I can do that tomorrow. Good idea. I really want to get to the bottom of Debbie's agenda."

"And are there other Assistant Editors that you can speak with as well?"

"Yes! There is Emily as well! I'll find her, too!"

Rachel slept restlessly that night since there was a lot on her mind. But she felt comfortable in that she knew how she was going to address her questions the following day. The problem was she had no idea what the answers would be.

Dan was able to work from home in the morning, so he stayed with Chloe. This allowed Rachel to get to work early as she knew between her project and the discussions she would need to have, she had a long day coming.

Rachel arrived a little before 7:00 a.m. and got right to work. By the time many of the other staff started to arrive around 9:00 a.m., she was much farther ahead than she thought she'd be. And as Rachel was reviewing her work, she was proud of what she had accomplished in a short period of time. She knew that Michael wanted to check in with her regarding her progress at 11:00 a.m., so she decided to wait until then to explore Debbie's concerns with him.

"Hey, Rachel?" Michael poked his head in her office.

She looked up from her work and smiled. "Hey, Michael. Come in!"

"Is now a good time? I'm sure you're really busy."

"Nothing I haven't handled before," Rachel said confidently.

"This is quite the curveball to someone so new here. How are you handling the workload relative to the deadline?"

"It's not too bad. I've done this kind of work before. So it's getting to know how the company does things, not the actual work. Does that make sense?" Rachel thought it did.

"It sure does. Every company is different," Michael smiled. He knew she would be good hire when he met her.

"I have a question for you. This deadline change was a pretty big one. Does it happen often?" Rachel assumed she was being smooth with the question.

"Every now and then it does. Honestly, the company that does our printing doesn't always have their act together. We have our deadlines of when we would like to get the magazines published and distributed. And then the printer gives us the dates they need our files by so they can print them on time. But too many times the printer doesn't seem to care to abide by the deadlines they set which, unfortunately, make us change our deadlines to fit their schedule. I've been pushing upper management to look for a new printer. But the costs this company gives us are so good, they are hesitant to make a change."

"Wow, so this may happen again next month?" Rachel was surprised by Michael's candor.

"Unfortunately, yes. I would say it happens a few times a year and rarely on consecutive months. But I wouldn't rule anything out."

Michael stood up to leave.

"It looks like you have everything under control. Really impressive. Some of our staff have a really hard time managing these shifting deadlines."

"What do you mean?" Rachel thought Michael opened the door to discuss the issue.

"Let's just say that some staff think I'm the problem. And no matter how often I may explain otherwise, they still believe I'm the problem."

"Good to know," Rachel wanted to end it there. "I appreciate you checking in with me."

"Let me know if you need anything," Michael stood and left the office.

Rachel was surprised by Michael's candor. Obviously things were frustrating to him as well. But it seemed like his hands were tied and everyone had to do deal with the problem. Now she was really curious to speak with Emily to gather her perspective as well.

After lunch, Rachel wandered down the hall to Emily's office. She had met her briefly during orientation, but she hadn't yet settled enough into her role to get to know her.

"Excuse me, Emily?" Rachel peered around the door frame to passively interrupt her colleague.

"Yes?" said Emily without looking away from her screen.

"I'm Rachel, the new Assistant Editor. We met briefly during orientation? I just wanted to come by and introduce myself again."

"Oh, yes! Hi!" Emily immediately stopped what she was doing and rose to shake Rachel's hand.

"Some change with the deadline, huh?" Rachel cut to the chase.

"I know. This stupid printer. I don't know why we still work with that company."

"That's what I heard. How does the change in deadline affect everyone else?" Rachel was hoping not to mention Debbie's name first.

"Well, everyone is pretty used to it. Except Debbie. She hates when this happens."

Rachel's ears perked up. "Does she usually get frustrated?"

"Always. Although now I think I'm actually starting to agree with her. It's so frustrating to have these crazy deadline shifts at a moment's notice all of the time. I think she wants us all to talk with Michael's boss, Erin, about it after we meet the new deadline."

"I heard about that. What's your thought?" Rachel figured questions wouldn't hurt.

"Well, Debbie has clout. She and Erin go way back. I am frustrated by all of this. I think I'll take her side. I just don't think it's worth the possible repercussions in the future."

"I can see that. I'm new, so I was just trying to understand where everyone was coming from."

"Best advice I can give is not to cross Debbie. She has a way of making life difficult. Anyway, I have to get back to work. Let's grab a drink after work soon."

"Sounds good. Thanks for your help."

Rachel walked back to her office and stared at her screen. She was just unsure of what to do next. From what Emily said, she was going to go along with Debbie's plan mainly because she didn't want to deal with Debbie. And it sounded like Debbie can make people's lives miserable if they didn't agree with her. But Emily also seemed pretty passive. Rachel did wonder if she could handle it. She really didn't want to sit in a meeting with her boss' boss after one negative experience in a new company. But she also understood that not going may create some unwanted friction with her new colleagues.

Rachel tabled the thought until she arrived home from work later that night.

"So, how'd it go?" Dan asked.

"Interesting," Rachel responded as she plopped on the couch. She grabbed a cold slice of pizza that Dan had ordered much earlier in the evening. Their daughter had been asleep for some time.

"It turns out Debbie is a pain in the ass and people are scared of her. Emily, the other editor, is passive, and it sounds like she's going to go along with Debbie's plan to talk to Erin." Rachel paused. "I spoke with Michael. He seems to think I'm doing really well, and expressed his frustrations about the whole printer scenario as well. After speaking with him and Emily, I just don't think going to this meeting with Debbie is the right thing for me to do. Not after being there six weeks."

"I agree with you. I think it could really hurt your reputation quickly if you went into this meeting complaining. From what you said, it sounds like Michael appreciates your work, and that's not a perception you want to ruin. But what do you think Debbie will do if you don't go along with her?"

"That makes me nervous. She's pretty riled up. I would think that it would make our working relationship difficult. I guess I'll just have to trust that if it gets too hard, that I can lean on Michael for help. Ideally, I'll continue to prove myself and make it easy for him to have my back."

"It's a tough situation. But I think you're right," Dan agreed. "This is all supposed to happen tomorrow?"

"Yes. We've all dropped everything, so we should meet the deadline at about 3:00 p.m. I'm sure Debbie will want to go in right after our work is submitted."

"Well, let's see how it goes."

Rachel arrived at work early again to be sure she finished up her work and had time to proofread it. The day was surprisingly uneventful until about 2:00 p.m., when Debbie came to her office.

"So, I didn't hear from you. Emily agrees with me. Are you coming then? I set a time to meet with Erin at 4:00 p.m."

Rachel felt the tension in her chest, and her heart started to race.

"You know, I've been thinking about it. I don't think I'm going to join you. I just haven't been here long enough to form an opinion yet," Rachel concisely stated her case.

"But we need you to come. They're just going to keep taking advantage if we all don't go in together," Debbie started pressing.

"I get what you're saying. It would be different if I had more experience here, but I'm new and really don't want to get caught up in something this big when I don't even know yet what I'm supposed to be upset about," Rachel pushed back.

"This is really disappointing, Rachel. You know magazines. I thought you had experience. I have some clout here, and if this goes the way I'm hoping it will, you won't be here long," Debbie issued a not-so-subtle threat.

Debbie swiftly left Rachel's office. The only way Rachel could interpret Debbie's comments was that she was hoping she could convince Erin to fire her, or that she would somehow take Michael's job and then Debbie would let her go directly. Rachel began to reconsider her decision. She didn't want to be on Debbie's bad side. However, participating in this meeting was not a good idea either. Her heart was still racing. Rachel looked at the clock: 2:30 p.m.

She took a deep breath.

Then another one.

One more.

"Okay," Rachel thought to herself. If she waited it out, there was much more risk to her to show up to that meeting than not. Not showing up would clearly show that she was not aligned with Debbie, that she was focused on her work, and had a desire to be a good team player rather than a disruptive one. This thought process was enough for her. Rachel decided to stick with her original decision and not participate.

Erin's office was few doors down from Rachel's. At 4:00 p.m., Rachel poked her head out just as Debbie walked in to Erin's office, with Emily trailing behind. Neither Debbie nor Emily saw her. The door closed.

Rachel could only assume what was being discussed. Pretty quickly she could hear Debbie's voice rising with the tone being firm and harsh. It would be quiet for a moment (Rachel presumed Erin or Emily was speaking then). And then Debbie would resume. Since she had met the deadline, Rachel decided to leave a little early. Erin's door was still closed. Rachel was sure she would hear about the conclusion one way or another the next day.

This time Dan was going to be home late as he was caught on a work project. Rachel made Chloe dinner, bathed her, and put her to bed. She put on a TV show that she knew she was too tired to watch, and fell asleep quickly.

In the morning, she woke up in her bed with no recollection of Dan coming home, waking her up, or recalling her discussion about planes flying around the apartment. She and Dan had a good laugh about that before Dan dropped Chloe off at day care, and they both went to work.

Rachel opened the door to her office and was turning on the office lamps when there was a knock at her door even though it was already open. She turned and saw Michael and Erin.

"Mind if we come in?" Michael asked.

"Not at all! Please," Rachel motioned to the chairs in her office and the three of them sat down.

"I'm sure you know Debbie and Emily came to my office yesterday," Erin began.

Rachel nodded. Her heart rate was picking up again. Rachel wanted to listen carefully before she made any comments.

"Needless to say, it didn't go very well. Michael and I met this morning and we thought we should find you since you decided not come with them. Debbie said that she said she asked you to join them, but didn't know why you ultimately did not attend," Erin continued. "So, why didn't you go with them?"

Rachel was nervous. She wanted to answer the question but also didn't want to judge her colleagues in an unfair way. "Well, Debbie told me what her concerns were when the deadline was moved. I just didn't think after being here a short period of time, it was my place to make a judgment or complaint about how Michael runs the department, especially without speaking with him directly first."

Erin and Michael glanced at each other and were silent for what felt like minutes to Rachel, but was most likely only seconds.

Erin spoke again. "I have to ask you a question, and it needs to stay confidential."

Rachel nodded.

"Did Debbie threaten you at all?"

Rachel didn't know what to say. She hated the last interaction that she had with Debbie, but at the same time she didn't want to just throw her under the bus. But her bosses were sitting in front of her and asking the question, point blank. Rachel was scared to respond with the truth, but also was scared of what may happen if she wasn't truthful. Did they already know? Rachel didn't know what to say.

"Threaten seems to be a strong word," Rachel began, then paused. "Debbie more insinuated that things may not go well for me if I wasn't on her side." Rachel already felt like she said too much.

"Thank you for your honesty. Michael said you were a great hire. Your answer here cemented that for me," Erin responded, clearly impressed.

"That's all we wanted to discuss, Rachel, that you," Michael said as they stood up to leave.

"Okay," was all Rachel could muster as they left.

Rachel had no idea if the meeting went well or not. As her heart rate slowed and the queasiness subsided, she allowed herself to focus more on Erin's comments about being a good hire, rather than questioning the statements she made about Debbie. Regardless of how she was judging her comments about Debbie, clearly they were well received by Erin, which was all that mattered.

Rachel's day moved on uneventfully, until she heard some yelling in the hallway.

When Rachel stepped out of her office to see what was happening, she saw building security escorting Debbie out of her office. Debbie was carrying a cardboard box of her personal belongings. As security was walking her towards the elevator, Michael caught a glimpse of Rachel and started walking towards her. He motioned that they go into her office, which they did, and he closed the door.

"Sorry you had to see that," he said.

"I know it has to happen. None of my business why it did," Rachel responded. She didn't know what Michael was looking for.

"You're right. But, I'm sure you're putting two and two together and wondering if your comments contributed to what happened to Debbie."

Rachel saw Michael's eyes, and slightly nodded along with him.

Michael continued, "I just wanted you to know that Debbie has been, well, essentially a bully for too long around the office. We think many people resigned because of her. Erin and I really think highly of you, and if she had been bullying people, we didn't want you to leave because of her poor behavior and our inability to manage it. That's why we had to ask if something happened. The fact that you answered honestly gave our Human Resource Department all they needed to follow through in letting her go. I know that was hard for you to do, so thank you."

"I'm glad it wasn't just me," Rachel really did feel relieved. "I can understand."

Michael rose to leave, "All I can say is, 'Thank you.' I'm sure that was difficult. I'm glad you made the choice you did. Hopefully you'll enjoy your work here even more now."

As Michael left the office, Rachel immediately reached for her phone to tell Dan what had happened.

The Lesson

This story is an all too common example of interactions that occur in a workplace. Unfortunately, we can't control the behaviors of others in order to make us feel comfortable, but rather we must figure out how to control and manage our own. This story is about how adults who have successfully become adaptive and independent manage these situations effectively.

The first point is that, while Rachel managed things well, she didn't do it easily. She struggled. She was anxious. She was concerned about how her superiors may judge her. She worried about how her decisions may affect her relationship with her co-workers. It was difficult.

But she didn't avoid the anxiety, or just go along (like her co-worker Emily did), to make herself feel better. She challenged her anxiety. While she was worried about how she would be perceived by others, she didn't let the potentially negative perception that they may have of her influence her choice. She made the choice she did *despite* the potential repercussions that she identified, not because she was trying to avoid them.

And while all of this was going on, she focused on her work and scheduled herself accordingly to do the best work she could despite the circumstances. She didn't complain; she didn't become overwhelmed with the change; she just made the adjustments accordingly. And she did this while knowing full well that there was a major conflict brewing.

The story in and of itself isn't all that eventful. But that's also the point. When adults are able to be adaptive and independent, they are able to cut down on the "drama" that occurs in their lives and focus on doing the right things given the situations that they are in.

Diminishing the Drama

If we look more closely at Rachel, we can see that there were a number of areas where she could have been swallowed up by the workplace drama that was occurring.

First, if she wasn't able to manage the negative emotions of guilt or shame, she may have immediately taken Debbie's side in this argument. She would have been internally motivated to completely avoid the feelings of guilt that would have appeared should she decide to go against her. But instead, she was able to function independently, not initially taking any one person's side, but rather slowing down the pace of the interactions in order for her to make the decision possible for herself. Should she have been motivated by the avoidance of these negative emotions, Rachel would not have been able to think clearly about what had happened, and would have instead made choices to simply make the negative emotions disappear.

Being Positive Without Reinforcement

Rachel, clearly, was a confident and self-assured individual. She simply did not crave positive reinforcement from others. This trait made it much easier for her to remove herself from the situation in order to fairly assess the dynamic. If Rachel did have a strong need for consistent positive reinforcement, she would have had tremendous struggles in this situation. She would have felt the pressure to align with her co-workers because she would be concerned about the potential negative impact on their relationship if she didn't. Rachel also would have experienced tremendous pressure to align with her boss as his positive comments would have a significant impact on her career and job performance. This bind could have created an emotional situation for Rachel where she would have been completely torn about *whose side to take*, and would never have considered the possibility that taking no side was best for her.

That dilemma is a hallmark of those who crave positive reinforcement from their environment. They simply cannot handle operating independently. When people need external relationships to enhance their view of themselves, they are then unable to consider many other options of how to handle the circumstances they are in because their goal is purely one of "Who is going to be happiest with me?" when they make a decision, rather than "What is the best decision for me?" These are vastly different motives and goals, and clearly we can see how Rachel was able to look at her predicament from an alternative perspective. Rather than asking "Who is going to be happiest with me?", she intuitively knew that the best thing to do was not pick a side which, after speaking to her boss and coworker, led to her making the best decision for herself: Remaining neutral. Clearly the stance of remaining neutral had major benefits to her. But if she picked a strong side in one way or another, the underlying problem of Debbie being an office bully would never have come to light.

Taking the Long-Term View

Rachel also was fully aware that there was no easy solution to this problem, and that the consequences of her stance would not be limited to just this issue. Rachel and her husband spoke about how she had to consider the totality of her reputation, and how damage to that may have affected her employment going forward. Looking at the long-term view of how she may be perceived by others also contributed to her stance of remaining neutral. If Rachel looked short-term only, the benefit to her clearly would be to side with her coworkers. The change in deadline was incredibly frustrating. Short-term, the best decision was to push management to fix that problem. But there are long-term repercussions to all decisions, and when looking at the ramifications of a decision beyond the initial consequence, one can best evaluate how good a decision really is.

And this is where the phrase, "sometimes you have to lose the battle in order to win the war," comes in. In our personal or professional lives, we simply cannot fight every battle on our way to our long term goals. We have to choose what battles to lose in order to eventually win the war. When a person fights every battle because they know they're correct, and that it is "not fair" if other people get away with what they are doing, they will tire themselves out from fighting. And they'll lose lots of friends and colleagues in the process. In Rachel's case, in looking to the long term, she was inherently willing to deal with the hassle of the changing deadlines in order to build her work reputation and create her own identity at her new place of employment. Rachel was willing to lose the battle in the name of winning the larger war. Not being caught up in the desire for instant gratification allowed her to remain focused on the smarter, longer term decisions that would enhance her standing in the company appropriately.

Controlling, But Not Eliminating, Anxiety

Rachel also had full control of her anxiety. It's not that she didn't feel anxious, but she understood and controlled it. Too many times in people's lives, the anxiety is immediately overwhelming, and therefore they make decisions based on removing the anxiety. But that only provides short-term relief as people then don't think about the long-term ramifications of their decisions, and they may have to deal with the secondary issues that were created by them. **And somehow people also believe that controlling anxiety means not actually having anxiety. This just isn't true.**

Everyone will always have some level of anxiety all of the time. The issue is how to best monitor and understand why it exists. Rachel clearly knew why her anxiety existed, but she didn't judge herself for it. She didn't tell herself it was "stupid" to feel that way. She just remained focused on the issues in front of her, while needing to give her anxiety a little extra care periodically in order to keep it in check. Being self-aware and not intimidated by the emotions helped Rachel stay focused where she needed to: On making the best decision for herself.

If she were guided by anxiety, she would have first agreed with Debbie to support her, and then she would have been too scared about the consequences from Michael. She would have changed her mind about Debbie, only to have to deal with the repercussions of backing out from her. The wavering in the decision making would have created much drama in her life, and a tremendous obstacle to her making the best decision for herself.

Anxiety limits our ability to think clearly and independently. But, most destructively, it confuses us into thinking what the best *adaptive* decision really is. We may be confused into thinking that a decision to eliminate anxiety is the most adaptive one for us. But it's misleading. We'd be confusing an emotional decision that helps us *feel* better, with one that may actually make things better. They are not always one in the same. Which is why understanding and controlling anxiety is so important. It allows us to see that even though there may be a tempting decision that will allow us to feel better, it can also allow us to see that there may be another decision that won't completely remove the anxiety that is felt in the moment, but will the best for our own, long term prosperity.

Accepting Circumstances and Responsibility

And let's not discount the value of Rachel's personal life. Her young family was busy. But it was clear that they all accepted their circumstances and responsibilities, and they shared them all. Because of this, the hectic work schedules, caring for young child, and other responsibilities just didn't create emotional demands for them. Rachel and Dan were engaged, supportive, and understanding of what each had to do for the benefit of the family and themselves individually. This allowed for them to have difficult discussions, but also step back and, in this case, for Rachel to make her own decisions independently, without fear of being judged by her husband.

Now granted, there will be times that spouses argue and life gets hard. There's no way around that. But the foundation of the relationship should be one of mutual respect and trust. When this exists in a relationship, it makes it easier for the couple to function when there are challenges. If a relationship is based on one person having to feel positive about themselves or any other symptom of a spouses' insecurity, then that insecurity will only be exacerbated when a real conflict or significant life stress arises. At this point, the arguments that occur are now on two levels: The significant issue or life stress is the one that is spoken about, and comforting a spouse's insecurity or fear is the undertone. And the problem is that they both can't happen. Sometimes life stress creates insecurity. There is no way to make it better.

Living as an adult who is adaptive and independent doesn't happen by accident. It starts with a foundation of skills, taught at a young age. These skills are then cultivated throughout childhood and practiced in school and social relationships. As new adults coming into college and adult life, they can then be confident in the skills they have mastered.

Chapter 11

Next Steps

As a parent, it's easy to feel defeated at virtually every turn. Whether it's due to our guilt because we can't provide enough materially or emotionally for our children, or we feel like our kids aren't learning what they need to either academically or socially, or we don't know if our kids are involved in the "right" extracurricular activity, it seems there's always a problem that needs solving. And parents desperately feel like they need to remain afloat or, rather, keep their kids afloat. This is a perpetual battle that parents fight and their goal is just to cross the finish line (after high school) and move forward. Many parents are exhausted and worried. Because of their historical involvement in their children's lives, they struggle with letting them go to college or transitioning themselves to being empty nesters.

There are ways to combat this feeling as a parent, but it involves challenging the perspective and attitude that's somehow been ingrained by our culture about what it means to be a parent. Our culture values the over-protecting of our children and over-empathizing with our children. But just because our culture values these things, it doesn't mean that they're the best for our kids. Now, obviously, we don't want our kids to be physically or emotionally harmed in any way, but we also don't want to create fragile beings either. And therein lies the problem: Many parents believe that there's either one or the other and that they both cannot coexist together.

But as parents we must figure out how to have them coexist. If we err completely on the side of protecting our children, then we create fragile human beings. If we err on the other side of not wanting to create fragile humans, then we can create a child who becomes a narcissist or potentially a sociopath (individual who is void of empathy). But all of these traits are important, and our attitudes will determine how we communicate these things effectively. We aren't able to communicate the value of both unless we understand the value of both sides. Many parents dismiss the value of "hardening" their children in favor empathy because they want their children to be kind to others. That's a great idea, but it never plays out well in a practical sense.

For example, if a child in school is being bullied on the playground by one particular kid many days of the week, would you want your child to fight back or tell a teacher? Personally, I fall in the category of wanting the child to fight back, if the situation is not a threat to life or limb. And here's why: In adult life, there is no teacher, nor anyone else, who is going to come save an individual from their issue. I would rather my child learn the skill of standing up for themselves, and deal with the consequences of their actions, rather than telling a teacher so someone else can solve their problems. We teach our children to not fight, be respectful, be kind, and when another child isn't displaying those traits, we tell them to find an adult. And the child expects the adult to handle the situation and "fix it" so now the other child will act in a better way.

But there are many problems with this. First, the child who is trying to do the right things only knows that they can't solve a problem and that they need an adult to do it. When they get older, they will have limited practice solving their own conflicts because their only solution will have been to call in for help. Second, the child who is doing the wrong thing won't experience natural, social consequences to their actions. They may learn that acting in certain ways may get a teacher involved, but they won't necessarily learn that when they act a certain way, no one will play with them. And this is because of the first problem that too many children are trying to be nice. But by being too nice, they are not sticking up for themselves and they are not allowing other children to learn by experiencing real natural consequences to their actions.

That was a simple playground example. But let's expand this to young adulthood and dating. How does someone who is 16 to 23 years old and dating know if they should end a relationship? They should know when it intuitively or concretely "isn't right." But if nothing concrete happens, and they haven't been taught how to listen to intuition, how do they know? This is why many young women who I've worked with over the years struggle to end relationships that they may feel are "controlling" or "emotionally manipulative." They want to believe the best in the other person and want to trust them, but can't make the final decision that the relationship is not good for them. And they will say that many times it's because they'll "feel bad" if they cast that type of judgment. But it's exactly the judgment that they are supposed to cast! The problem is that they haven't done it often enough to get comfortable with understanding the reasons behind the choice, and why that choice would be necessary for them in that given situation. Consequently, they are many times emotionally harmed by their significant other until something "concrete" in nature does occur, like a violent outburst or other emotional abuse that is just too obvious to ignore. The situations should not progress that far, and teaching our children the skills to understand their emotions will help them avoid many abusive situations that too often occur.

The points I hear when speaking with parents about these issues are "That's too harsh," "How could you say that?" etc. But here's the reality: Teaching our kids to be nice, kind, respectful, caring and thoughtful to others is fantastic. It really is. They are great character virtues that will help them in their lives. But their value is only *maximized* when they come into contact with other people who share the same virtues. And in life, we can't guarantee that our kids will only come into contact with nice, kind people. Therefore it is absolutely incumbent on parents to teach their kids the other side of the "emotional coin."

And this "other side of the coin" is about them internally feeling capable of handling stress, anxiety, guilt, and shame. When they come into contact with the people who don't share their own respectful values, these other (we'll call them "bad") people will make them anxious, will generate stress, will be emotionally manipulative, and make them feel awful for things that they shouldn't. When our kids learn the "other side," they will be able to internalize a strong level of confidence and assurance in themselves to know that just because this "bad" person is making them feel anxious, they can also remind themselves to dismiss the feeling and reinforce to themselves that they are right, and not the bad person. Many people find themselves trying to resolve a situation by making the bad person feel better, when the reality is that this will never work. That bad person is an emotional "taker," and will just want more. There has to be a limit to emotional giving.

Just as there are bad people who will try to take advantage, there are also the individual choices and decisions that we all make. Let's look at a recent University of Chicago study, conducted by Steven Levitt. He found thousands of people who were struggling to decide upon a major life decision (accepting a marriage proposal, new job, etc.), and they agreed to leave the choice up to him. By a coin flip. Yes, a flip of the coin. Heads, they said "Yes, I'll do it," tails was "No, I'll decline." After he made the decisions for his participants, he followed up with the participants six months later to evaluate how happy the people were in their situation decided by the coin flip. The ones who had heads (said "yes" to question) were significantly happier than the average person who received "tails" (those who said "no").

There are two points to consider in this study. First, taking a risk isn't always a bad thing. By teaching our kids to consistently look through a lens of "safety and security," we're not doing a good job teaching them how and when to take risks. In my belief, it's why many people are happier when they were forced to take the risk and answer the question in the affirmative. Second, there were just too many people who even wanted to participate in this study in the first place. Again, this speaks to the sheer number of people who don't know how to read their own anxiety. They became so swallowed up in it that they had to turn to someone else—and a coin flip!—to make their decisions. This is not a way to live confident, assertive, adaptive, and independent lives.

Which is why, as parents, we have to start asking ourselves what's most important for our kids. In my view, as was illustrated in many of the stories written in the book, is that a parent must decide if their goal for parenting is for the short-term (through high school), or long-term (what happens in adulthood). And here's why I break it down in those terms.

If a parent has a goal only in the short term, they are going to want to ensure that their child has no conflict with other kids, does absolutely fantastic in school (at virtually all costs), and excels in their extracurricular activities. This will be because they want their child to look and be the best when they graduate high school. They want them to be accepted into an elite college.

If a parent has a long-term goal, they will be concerned with social development, academics, and how the child does in their extracurricular activities. But they won't define the child by it. The parents will also be concerned with their child's process of learning, and may even put greater weight on how their kids are learning, not only on whether or not they have learned.

Put simply, parenting to the short term is "outcomes driven parenting." Parents measure the success of their children based upon what they are achieving. And parents believe that measurements that indicate success will automatically translate into a successful adulthood.

Parenting to the long term not only focuses on what they are learning, but encompasses *why* they are learning it. It's why a parent may value a B in a class because of the process a student had to experience in order to obtain the B, over an A in another class where there wasn't a meaningful process in the learning. The intangible traits of motivation, determination, perseverance, combined with emotional intelligence and self-awareness, can create a successful adult. Parenting to the long term values the intangible just as much (if not more) than the tangible.

But this takes a great of amount of confidence from parents to believe that they are doing the right things by their children, by valuing the things that our culture and other parents would say just aren't valuable. And this is where many parents get swallowed up. They get consumed with our culture and out of fear, resort to the short-term strategies that most other parents subscribe.

Parents have to make a clear choice in their homes. They must answer the question as to whether they should parent for the short-term outcomes or real, long-term success. Most parents would say the answer should be both. But that's inherently wrong. The values are too conflicting in both points of view for them to be simultaneously true. Parents must decide how much emotional intelligence and self-awareness contributes to the success of adaptive, independent, and successful adults. If parents believe that an elite college, great GPA, or outstanding SAT score is a predictor of success for their kids, then they will parent to the short term. But, if their kids are successful, it will be because their child innately had the emotional intelligence to use their intellectual ability to its capacity.

If parents understand that self-awareness, emotional intelligence, perseverance, and other intangible traits need just as much nurturing and cultivation as the academic and intellectual development, they will accept that sometimes their children may struggle academically for the benefit of the emotional and treat that experience as being valuable and integral to their future success.

As you move forward at home, with all of the happy moments and unpleasant experiences life can throw at you, it's time to start asking the hard questions about what you value. Ask yourself questions such as:

> What do I need to teach my kids so that they can become adaptive and independent adults?
>
> What do I view as a success for my kids?
>
> What do I view as a failure?
>
> What do I expect of my kids and is this realistic?
>
> Who (as in, what type of person) do I want my child to become?

Many parents answer these questions in one way: Through outcomes. They will say good grades, internships, success in extracurricular activities. Most often, they don't incorporate intangible skills into their answer because they simply don't view them as valuable.

But these skills are much more valuable than anything they will learn in school. Patrick Lencioni, *New York Times* bestselling author, wrote a book called *The Ideal Team Player*. In it, he outlines that if adults can excel in three areas, they will thrive in any workplace. All of the skills incorporate an ability to be self-aware, adaptive, and independent. In my view (and in the view of countless studies), these skills will predict future success greater than test scores or the name of college attended. And that's ultimately the point of this book: For parents to understand that they can create a successful child by guiding them as they grow up to learn the emotional skills necessary that will allow them to be successful in their professional and personal lives as they enter adulthood.

References and Resources

Chapter 1:

Depression and Anxiety Journal. Association of Social Media Use and Depression Among US Young Adults (2016), University of Pittsburgh staff and students: Jaime E. Sidani, Ariel Shensa, Ana Radovic, Elizabeth Miller, Jason B. Colditz, Beth Hoffman, and Leila M. Giles

Social Cognitive and Affective Neuroscience Advance Access. "Willpower" Over the Life Span: Decomposing Self-Regulation (2010). Walter Mischel, Ozlem Ayduk, Marc G. Berman, B. J. Casey, Ian H. Gotlib, John Jonides, Ethan Kross, Theresa Teslovich, Nicole L. Wilson, Vivian Zayas, and Yuichi Shoda. https://web.stanford.edu/group/mood/docs120610/Mischel_SCAN_2010.pdf

Chapter 3:

Health Education Research, Volume 19, Issue 4, August 2004. Self Esteem in a Broad Spectrum Approach for Mental Health Promotion. Michal (Michelle) Mann Clemens M. H. Hosman Herman P. Schaalma, Nanne K. de Vries https://academic.oup.com/her/article-lookup/doi/10.1093/her/cyg041

Chapter 7:

Bruni, Frank. Where You'll Go Is Not Who You'll Be . March, 2015.

National Bureau of Economic Research NBER Working Paper No 7322 August 1999. Estimating the Payoff to Attending a More Selective College: An Application of Selection on Observables and Unobservables. Stacy Berg Dale, Alan B. Krueger http://www.nber.org/papers/w7322

Gladwell, Malcolm. David and Goliath. October, 2013.

CEO Genome Project, Published in *Harvard Business Review* May-June 2017 issue. Full book being published in 2018. Authors: Elena L Botelho, Kim R. Powell, Tahl Raz.

Next Steps:

National Bureau of Economic Research NBER Working Paper No 22487 August 2016. Heads or Tails: The Impact of a Coin Toss on Major Life Decisions and Subsequent Happiness. Steven D. Levitt. http://www.nber.org/papers/w22487

Lencioni, Patrick. *The Ideal Team Player*. April 2016.

About the Author

Adam Russo has been a Licensed Clinical Social Worker for over 15 years as well as having experience in various capacities in the mental health field for over 20 years.

He obtained his first experience in the mental health field by volunteering at Bellevue Hospital in New York City while in high school. How mental illness affected the many individuals he saw there was profound. Since then, he always had an interest in improving the mental health of others.

Adam earned his Bachelor of Arts degree in Psychology from Southern Methodist University in Dallas, Texas, and his Masters of Social Work from Smith College in Northampton, Massachusetts.

He has been an early intervention and prevention youth outreach worker where his role was to perform home and school visits to adolescents at risk of being involved in gangs, drug dealing, and violence.

Adam had since become a therapist in a residential placement setting for children who were in the system of the Department of Children and Family Services. The children in this setting had extremely severe emotional and behavior issues to the point that they were not able to live in a community setting and required placement in a facility that was equipped to manage their illness and behavior.

After being promoted on three separate occasions, Adam eventually started his own, outpatient, mental health center in 2006, Edgewood Clinical Services. Adam is currently the Chairman and CEO of the company. Edgewood Clinical Services currently has four locations, employs over 60 people, and provides the full range of outpatient mental care.

He was a featured speaker at TEDx Naperville with a presentation topic of: *We Must Teach Kids to Fail.*

He lives with his wife, of 17 years, Heather, and their three girls.

A Special Gift from Adam Russo

Now that you have your copy of *Unwritten Rules: Real Strategies to Parent Your Child to Success*, you can now feel secure that there is more than just test scores that determine the success of your child. It is a great benefit to be reinforced that *WHO* a child is, not what they accomplish, still matters.

You'll also receive a special bonus I created to add to your toolkit. It is a special Bonus Chapter that highlights the struggles that exist for kids who have a desire to focus on STEM (Science, Technology, Engineering, and Math), and how to combat them.

There's so much confusing information out there about parenting. When you finish this book you'll be armed with what you need to know to see through the "noise" and focus on the issues that really matter to you, as the parent.

You can claim your special bonus for free here:

https://www.adamrussobooks.com/hiddenchapter

The sooner you know what the most important issues are for you, as the parent, to focus on with your child, the better your chances to raise your child into a successful adult.

I'm in your corner. Let me know if I can help further.

Best,

Adam Russo